The New Guy Code

Becoming a Man in a Fatherless Society

Tony A. Gaskins Jr.

I hope this
book blesses
you!!

Library of Congress Cataloging-in-Publication Data

Tony A. Gaskins Jr.,
The New Guy Code: Becoming A Man In A Fatherless Society
Edited by: Jenna Cabbell
Published by: Soul Writers, LLC:
PO Box 291835 Tampa, FL 33687

ISBN: 978-0-9844822-9-0
10 9 8 7 6 5 4 3 2 1

Printed in the United States of America

Note: Readers are advised to consult a professional therapist,
counselor, or life coach before making any changes in their life.
The reader assumes all responsibility for the consequences of
any actions taken based on the information presented in this
book. The information in this book is based on the author's
research and experience. Every attempt has been made to
ensure that the information is accurate; however, the author
cannot accept liability for any errors that may exist. The facts
and theories on life, love and relationships are subject to
interpretation, and the conclusions and recommendations
presented here may not agree with other interpretations.

WARNING!!!

This book presents some very harsh and real truths. This book can be depressing and overwhelming as all of our societies problems are presented. There are parts of the book that provide instructions and solutions to our problems and hopefully will help you recover from the blows in the first half of the book. If you are easily offended please do not read any further than this page. If you struggle with hearing the truth of others please do not read any further than this page. The problem is much bigger than the solution because the solution is much more simple than the problem. In this book I focus on describing the problem because it's taken me many years to fully understand it myself. The solution is very simple. ACCEPT RESPONSIBILITY! That's it. This book is written for the eyes of men only! So if you are a female reading this book please realize that the language is very straightforward and real because it is meant to be a man-to-man conversation. Please beware that by reading this book you are peeping in on a conversation that isn't designed for you so please take no offense. To the men, if you are open to change and the perspective of others then this book will bring help and healing to a lot of the issues we face in our world today.

Contents

Introduction

There is a decline occurring in our society. The mindset of men is shifting drastically and the men of our past are becoming almost unrecognizable. What are we to do? I can't speak for everyone but I want my children to have men to look up to and admire. I want the quality of man to increase instead of decrease. I want my daughter to be swept off her feet by a man with class. I want my son to be able to make decent friends and not resort to being a loner because he has values and morals. I can speak on this issue because I once was what I call a "grown boy." I coined that term some years back and I use it often, so get accustomed to it. A "grown boy" is an adult male who has childlike tendencies and behaviors. At the age of twenty-five, I really became a man. By that time, I had already been married and a father for two years. In this society, I was moving pretty fast. Today, I look around and I can barely hold an intelligent conversation with some men 10 years older than me. I can't even fathom seeing eye-to-eye on the issues of manhood with a lot of guys my age. There are too few real men in our world and that must change. Today, I know and recognize what a real man is because

I've become one. I understand what it takes to become one because I come from one of the worst places a man can be in his life—I was one of the worst and now I've become one of the best. If anyone understands the journey into manhood, it's me. Imagine a man who had slept with over 100 women by the age of twenty-two. I once was a man who was a thief, drug-dealer and a toxic boyfriend. I once was a man who couldn't be trusted beyond your eyesight. Some could say, "Oh, but you were just a child." But no, I was an adult, and an irresponsible adult is a danger to our society. Today, I am a devout Christian, a faithful husband, a loving father, a high six-figure purpose-driven entrepreneur, and a law-abiding citizen. I made it from being a "grown boy" and became a grown man. If I can do it, then any man can. This is why I want to help, because I understand. Our men need men who will set examples and lead. Our men need new role models and real lessons on manhood. Our society needs fathers and not just "baby-daddies." Our children need parents and not parents who want to be the child's best friend. Our world needs a makeover. I believe it starts with the man. Let's become real men in this society and begin to change our world.

I
Find Yourself

This will be the most important thing you do as a man. When I found myself, it changed my life. I saw myself differently, I saw the world differently, and I began to love differently. The reason why most men have such a hard time finding their way in the world is because they are looking for ways the world can serve them instead of ways they can serve the world. When I was looking for ways to make money, I was miserable and desperate, but when I looked within and started giving back to the world, my life changed.

When I was about 19 years old, I started selling drugs from my dorm room. I was looking for significance in the world and also to make some fast money. I thought the drug dealers were tough and real men because they took chances and had the balls to risk their freedom. After the drug dealing, I got into the multi-level marketing companies because they sold a dream of overnight wealth and the idea of being one's own boss. I quickly found out that I'd have to work extremely hard and that it's really tough trying to sell people on something everyday that really won't change their lives. You're selling legal insurance, but how often will a normal person need a letter written from a lawyer? You're selling shakes, but are they FDA approved and have you tried them yourself for at least five years to see if they have any adverse effects on your body? You're selling used cars that you know will break down in a few months. You're selling coffee that you know will end up working against a person's health instead of being beneficial for them. You're selling drugs that will ruin someone else's life and also your own when you're caught. You're showing up at a job every day that you hate, but you feel like it's the only thing out there for you. All of these things we get sucked into for the wrong reasons, and then we find ourselves stuck. Even if you happen to find a job that has some type of intrinsic value working for someone else, you will still long for more in life. The reason why is because each one of us is created for a specific purpose and to give back to the world from our personal gifts, and at some point or in some capacity, to be our own bosses.

Ask yourself, what are my gifts? What do I do exceptionally well that not everyone else can do just as well? With that gift, how can I inspire or be a blessing to others? If the gift won't necessarily be a blessing to others, then what cause do I care about that I can offer some of my time and money? Those are the key questions to finding your purpose in life.

Get a pen and pad and write those questions and answers down. Then identify a business for your gift. The question is: How can I monetize my gift? How can I sell my gift to the world? This isn't as easy as it sounds, so I'll tell you my story on how I found myself.

I had always known how to express myself in writing. I was very quiet and shy for the most part, but when I got a pencil in my hand, I could do some serious damage to that paper. I was running from my natural gifts and trying to do the things where I saw others become successful. I played football in college. I sold drugs in college. I robbed in college. I sold legal insurance in college. I sold milkshakes. I worked at a group home. I worked in a grocery store. I worked in a warehouse. I tried so many things but ignored my natural gift of writing and expressing myself with profound wisdom. Then finally at 22 years old, I decided to write a book. It only took me about 10 days to write the book. It felt so good to write. I used a search engine to research how to publish a book. I went with the first company that popped up. It cost me $1,300 total to publish the book. I created a website by myself for $15. I printed up business cards for $150. I was ready to go. My book didn't do what I thought it would do. My first royalty check was only $300. I was disappointed. I returned to selling drugs, but that made my wife leave me. So I let the drug dealing go to get my wife back and I decided to go full-fledge in the book world. I set a goal to get onto The Oprah Winfrey Show, and I pitched myself daily for two years straight. Finally, Oprah invited me as a guest to tell my story. Shortly after, I made it to The Tyra Banks Show and then The 700 Club. The next year, I gained popularity on Twitter and people saw the picture of me with Oprah. They started emailing me invites to speak. The year after my appearance on The Oprah Winfrey Show, I earned around $10,000 speaking, and I was still working a regular job, so I couldn't complain. I had a lot of wisdom for a young man, so as people started writing in about my book and my tweets, I told them I was a Life Coach and I charged $25 an hour. I was speaking, coaching and working a regular job. My job wasn't fulfilling at all, but using my natural gifts was very gratifying.

One thing led to the next. I started my company, Soul Writers, LLC, and I earned income through that company to speak, life coach, ghostwrite and consult. I completed my first ghostwriting project for free. The next one, I charged $1,000, and the next one, I charged $1,500. I just kept going. I started charging $500 to teach others how to write and publish their own books. My business was picking up. In 2011, I got an investor. He saw my brand and how my following was growing online, and he saw my earning potential. He invested $15,000 more than what my day job paid me in a year. That allowed me to walk away from my day job for a year. I vowed that in that year, I'd do so much business that I'd never have to go back. I marketed myself daily and I paid attention to every lead. That year with the investor, I ended up bringing in over a quarter million dollars to my company, and some of that paid me. I continued to speak, coach, consult and ghostwrite. The following year, I was all on my own. My investor's money was all invested, and none of it had made a return yet, but my brand and business was growing. The year of faith where I was all alone, I made six figures just using my natural gifts. I had books in the publishing industry, and I was speaking, coaching, consulting, ghostwriting, and teaching group classes. I put my products out in many different forms and I continued to dream. I earned six figures without even realizing it. There wasn't a month in that year that I made under $8,000. I must let you know that when I was working for someone else and not using my gifts, I never made more than $1,800 in a month. Now my lowest month was $8,000, and my big months could be around $20,000. What was I doing? I was using my gifts. I realized that God has given us gifts that can make us a living if we are dedicated to using them. God didn't create a university, man did. So you have to know that what you need to succeed is already inside of you. You just have to be willing to use your gifts. Every man can write a book of lessons from his life just as I've done. Every man has a passion of some sort. Every passion can bring a profit. Every passion can serve a purpose. You have to find yourself.

After I started living my purpose and using my gifts to better the lives of others, my life elevated to another level. My life went to another level because my mind went to another level. Today, I feel too big to sleep with a random girl. I feel too big to cheat on my wife. I feel like too much of a man to yell or curse at my wife. I feel like too much of a man to walk out on my kids. I feel like too much of a man to lie, cheat or steal. My purpose has set me free. My purpose has given me a platform that I never want to fall from, so I govern my life accordingly.

If I can do it, then you can do it. It was a total of five years from the time I wrote my book until the time I made six figures. It was four years from the time I published my book until the time I was able to walk away from my job where I worked for someone else. That's not a long time at all. I believe you can do the same and even better.

Once you identify your purpose and become your own boss, your life will change for the better. That's not the only thing you need though. What's most important is that you realize a higher power created you. You were not created on your own. You are not self-made; you are God-made. It is imperative that you seek God. Read your Holy Bible daily. Get the messages from that book and do everything in your power to live by the teachings of the Holy Bible. That is what gave me the intangible things I need to succeed in life. Being accountable to God and knowing your place on this Earth will give you so much clarity in your life. I grew to trust God and to believe in Him wholeheartedly, and since that time, I haven't wanted for anything. Every month, my bills are paid and my needs are met. God answers my prayers and I keep His commandments. Having that accountability keeps me focused, stable and hungry. I know God is real because I've tried Him at His Word. God doesn't bless mess; He blesses a real effort from a willing heart. I'm not living in sin and expecting God to move on my behalf. I'm living a righteous lifestyle and He is answering my prayers and ordering my footsteps.

I found myself full when I surrendered to God's orders for life. I realized that He is my creator and that His book is the hand guide for life. It's the realest book ever written and I'm a living witness of that fact. I dare you to try it! When I say, "try it," I mean to live your life like Christ lived His. Cut out everything that is unrighteous. Live your life as if Jesus himself is sitting right next to you in the physical. Many men don't ever reach their full potential because they are never willing to live like that. Many men look at me and wonder what's special about me that allows me to have my kind of past and be as country and simple as I am but known around the world and making six figures living my dreams. I'm able to do these things because I live my life as if Jesus is sitting next to me in the physical. I live a pure and holy life, and I reap the promises that God's Word tells me I will. I dare you to try it, and I guarantee you that your actions will not be in vain. When I sin, I sin in front of Jesus, and when I repent, I repent wholeheartedly with the intention to not do it again. Even though I may slip up daily and lust after a woman who walks by me with a nice body, I ask for forgiveness and I start over fresh and new. God's grace is sufficient and He meets my needs. I dare you to try Him. That's the only guarantee that I can make to you. If you try God, He will not fail you. Many men make money and set records but have no peace and happiness because they don't have a relationship with Christ. Many men are married but don't know how to love and lead their wives because they have no relationship with Christ. Many men are frustrated and have tried everything in their power to succeed but still fail because they have no relationship with Christ. I dare you to try Him! He won't fail you!

Find yourself my brother!! Your life will never be the same.

II

The Misconceptions of Manhood

The way we were raised:

As boys, we are shown so many images of manhood. Unfortunately, we don't yet have the filters in our brains that throw out the junk images and keep the good ones. We absorb it all and these conflicting images cloud our minds and our judgment. Not every young man in a single parent home is a bad person or bringing our society down. There are some great single parent homes in our world. So many of the young men without fathers in the home hurt more than the average individual, and that inside pain causes them to do things that they don't really desire to do. That bravado, machismo, or whatever you'd like to call it often pushes that young man to a point of no return. He becomes the go-to guy. He becomes the pack leader. He's leading out of fear and pain, but those emotions can make a young man dangerous. Those emotions become so strong and much stronger than the young men operating out of love, peace and self-assurance. This broken young man becomes the leader and everyone else follows.

Even in many two parent homes, young men are raised to suck up all pain, embrace it, and not to show it. "Get up! Shut up! Wipe your tears! Don't explain anything! Go on! Be a man! Suck it up!" That's all we hear, whether it is at home, at school or at practice. In essence, we are shaped to be dumb jocks that have no expression or emotion. A man like this will internalize pain for years and then explode on his girlfriend in a dorm room while in college. Then it transforms into a new habit, and that (new habit) is to annihilate anything that causes us to get angry. We began to survive and thrive on fear and pain. We ruin anyone with whom we are at odds, whether it is emotional, verbal or physical. Hurt people hurt people. That's what we become and it ruins us and everyone around us. If we don't run through the things we see as obstacles with violence, then we run from them with irresponsibility. This is why there are so many single mothers today.

You see, many young men have this picture of a man being like a steel vault. That vault is locked tight and maybe only one person has the code. That person may be a father that we've never met or a father that will never care to open that vault. That person may be a woman that we will ruin before she ever gets the chance to open the vault. That person may be Jesus Christ that we run from because we fear change and accepting responsibility. We've been told that a man is tough and that he has no feelings and emotions. We've been told that a man fights his way through everything and it's not worth talking about. We've been told that a man must be cold, harsh, and tough with life because life will never be easy on us. Even as athletes we've been told to annihilate our opponent and then step on his chest when he's down and out of breath. And if we are losing, then we must fall on our own sword rather than accept defeat. Our lessons on manhood have shaped our culture as men and created beings that fold under pressure and shy away from all real responsibility. We seek a thrill and competition, but we have no boundaries or limits, so therefore we self-destruct. Yes, I'm speaking of the extreme but this extreme is becoming next to normal. Right now, as men, we are lost. Our focus is 90 mph in one direction, and most often, we neglect everything else. Balance is a foreign concept. Responsibility to our loved ones is seen as being a loser or being a punk. Loving one woman is for squares and lames, we're told. Marriage is of the old days and isn't necessary today. Our women are seen as the enemy and not our allies. They are to be treated as footstools instead of as our ribs or the backbone. Our focus is money and the things it can buy instead of health and the wealth of things that money can't buy. We've been lied to. We've been tricked. We've been led astray, used and abused. What we call a man today is actually a "grown boy." He's an adult male who throws a tantrum when he doesn't get his way. He's a selfish kid on the playground of the world that wants it his way and only his way. He's a thrill-seeking child that has no regard for safety and structure in his life. Anything goes—whether it's smoking, drinking, gambling, fornication, adultery, pornography, profanity, abuse, lies, manipulation, shady business and winning at all costs. My friend, we are lost.

I remember growing up and seeing images of what I thought were men. Although I had a father in the home who came home every night, clothed me, and fed me, the majority always seemed to win. We do have some good men in the world. Unfortunately, most of the men who read this book may not really need all of it, but the men who do need it may never pick it up. We need for the majority of men to be good men and that's how we will win. I remember seeing my father's example of manhood, but it was overshadowed by what I saw in the world. I saw guys with the pants hanging low, smoking cigars, cursing, fighting, sleeping with women and counting a lot of money. I saw guys who would fight if they were looked at the wrong way. I saw guys in big fancy cars decorated with big, shiny rims. I saw guys with gold teeth, long goatees, or some fashion statement that set them apart. I saw guys inked with lots of tattoos. I saw guys with different girls every week or every month. I heard guys talking about the way they were getting fast money. Most of the time, it was from stealing from someone, robbing a business or selling drugs. I saw the attention from the girls that they got because of this fast money and criminal lifestyle. I saw the nice clothes, shoes and jewelry they had that neither I, nor my parents, could afford. I thought that was what being a man was all about. It makes you ask yourself some questions like: why would I be with one woman when I can have many? Why would I waste time in school all my life when I can sell drugs or steal and get away with it and make more money than people make on their jobs? Why would I wear khakis and tuck my shirt in and have my pants on my waist when the girls like the guys with the sagging pants, big shirts, flashy jewelry and wads of money in their pockets. Why would I listen to gospel music when everyone I know looks up to the rappers and loves hip-hop? Everyone dresses like his or her favorite rapper or celebrity. The music that's praising God is seen as boring and un-cool. The music that's degrading my sister and telling me to sell crack rock or have a wicked jump shot is what people love. Is everything my parents teaching me outdated? Are my parents setting me up for failure? Do my parents even know what cool is? Do I really want to behave like my parents around my peers who behave completely different?

I saw so much around me and accepted it as normal. It shaped my thoughts and actions. It sent me on a wild goose chase searching for myself. I was "lost and found" and then "lost and found" again and again. I didn't know whether I was coming or going. I could be one thing in the public eye and then be another in private. The pain of being something you're not is nearly unbearable. Deep down, I just knew I wasn't the only one. I remember being one of the only people I knew with two parents in the home. I began to feel ostracized and unrightfully privileged. I became ashamed of the fact that I had two parents. I remember begging my parents not to come to every game because the other kids' parents couldn't make it to see them play. I remember telling my father that I wish I were in a single-parent home because there's no way I'd be respected in the NBA if I came from a two-parent home. We think only the children of single-parent homes struggle, but in our society today, the children of two-parent homes suffer as well. I was afraid to be smart. I was afraid to be strong. I was afraid to be gifted beyond measure. I was afraid to be privileged. I was *ashamed* to be privileged. I wanted to be normal. I wanted to be illiterate. I wanted to be hood, ghetto and accepted. That was the normal. We didn't call it that, but now as an adult, I realize that's what it's called. Many of the people who grew up in places like mine may not still to this day realize that's what it's called. The culture almost makes you hate yourself; the hip-hop culture in particular. Many will label it what they want but if they're honest about it, there was nothing empowering about that culture other than for the individuals making the money. I had several friends who graduated high school not knowing how to read or write. I had several friends who never met their fathers. I had several friends who had never gone to church. I had several friends who never had two parents at any events in their lives, even if they knew both parents. My friends cursed since elementary school, had sex since middle school and smoke and drank all through high school. That was the culture. That was the mindset. Every race was divided even though we were integrated, and if you crossed that line, you weren't seen as your own race anymore. If you were black and hung with whites, you were an Uncle Tom. If you were white and hung with blacks, you were white trash or a "wigga." Because of this culture, I was forced to be someone that I wasn't. In fact, I started wanting to be something that I'm really not. To this day, I speak with a very strong southern accent because my grandmother was from Alabama and spoke very different from my teachers. My teachers represented education and advancement. My grandmother represented the struggle, hard work, humility, and also the short end of the stick. I wanted to be like my grandmother because I reasoned that talking like my white teachers probably would have made me a sellout. So I accepted broken English, bad grammar, and it became a habit that I still struggle with even today.

Because being cool was the opposite of school, illiteracy became the norm and was promoted and spread. Yes, we were descendants of slaves living in racist central Florida and that played a part as well. Yes, we were mental slaves and suffering from a domino effect in our society, and no, we didn't know how to reverse it at the time. Well guess what? I've finally figured it out and this is why I'm writing this book, with my illiterate, uneducated, country-bumpkin self. Everything that I thought I was supposed to be was a lie that had been passed down. Every image I saw of manhood was actually "grown boys" perpetuating a vicious cycle. The things I accepted as normal were actually abominations to God.

Through observation, I learned that being a man meant taking shortcuts in life. It meant demeaning, controlling and abusing women. It meant making bad choices and then trying to escape the consequences. It meant getting a woman pregnant out of irresponsibility and then leaving her to fend for herself because you aren't man enough to provide for her and your child. It meant defending your stance at all cost. It meant blaming everyone else for your choices, decisions and consequences, and never—under any circumstances—should you accept responsibility for your own actions. That's what being a man was according to my observations. That's what I saw, and that's what I strived to be without even knowing it.

III
The Trickle-Down Effect

How it affects our kids:

The idea of manhood has been broken down, polluted and diluted to the point that it's almost extinct. I never met either one of my grandfathers because even by their time period, the downward spiral in lifestyle had become so drastic that they died at early ages due to poor choices and habits. The idea of manhood had already begun to decline. I know nothing about a great-grandfather because my parents never met their grandparents either. I only knew my grandmother, and there wasn't much she could teach me in the way of being a man because she didn't know many. I'm not sure if this is just a black thing, but even if it is, it will soon become a universal problem. The black race endured a struggle that is hard to put into words even for the most articulate beings. The breakdown of the race, the division, the separation, and the engrained belief system was so demoralizing that one can only dream that we will be able to reverse this. Blacks are still emerging from the ashes though. Many blacks rise to power and wealth and have positive influence on the culture, but unfortunately, their influence is usually much less impactful than the pop-culture artists and TV personalities they are up against.

This trickles down to our young men, and each generation grows worse than the one before. With each passing year, our moral compass gets weaker and our rebellion gets stronger. The "good" is seen as bad and the "bad" is seen as good. God and all His wonderful power is being taken for granted in our society. People use His name in vain and blaspheme His name in music. The respect that our society once had for God is deteriorating at a rapid and saddening pace. Many rappers are mocking the church, mocking gospel music, mocking God, and not counting the cost. They are playing with their own lives and leading millions astray and not once reconsidering their actions. They're treating God as if He's a fairytale and as if He wasn't the backbone of our people at one point. Our generation is turning its' back on God and we are seeing all sorts of lawlessness in society. They've taken prayer out of schools. The Democratic Party even had to vote on whether or not they would use the name God at their convention. Next, we may take God out of our pledge to the American flag and Christians may soon suffer persecution in subtle forms. Do you recognize this happening in society? If so, are you afraid to speak up? Are you afraid to lose your job? Are you afraid to step on some toes? Are you afraid to lose some business? Are you afraid to stand up for the strong beliefs that were instilled in you as a youth? Many people *are* afraid. Many people are changing their values and morals to fit in with society. They are going with the flow and labeling it "growth and progress" when in all actuality, we are moving backwards. Although our country was never perfect, there were some beliefs that we stood on that had our nation in a much better position. Today, we are a weakened society and only getting weaker. We must confront this issue and be prepared to make a change. You have to trust and know that God will provide for your needs and take care of you for standing for what you believe. The road to destruction is always the most travelled. Beware of where you're headed, and turn back if you realize that it's in the wrong direction.

Our young men are embracing everything that is wrong and ignoring what's right. The voices of the sound individuals are often drowned out. We see a fatherless young man grow up and then make his own child a fatherless child. That cycle continues. It's deemed normal. The male forces himself to hate the woman who bore his child in order to sleep at night knowing that he's not accepting the responsibility that he brought into the world. Now we have grown men in their 30's and 40's teaching from the mindsets of a teenage boy and calling it wisdom. We have fatherless men leading fatherless kids and other fatherless adults into a place of ignorance. When I say fatherless, I don't mean all individuals reared in single-parent homes. I repeat, I am not speaking of all individuals raised in single-parent homes. By fatherless, I am referring to the unlearned and unwilling to learn. I mean individuals conceited in their own wisdom, whether raised in a two-parent home or a single-parent home. Today, we have the blind leading the blind. I've witnessed adult men teaching and condoning violence against women, abandonment of women, anti-marriage rhetoric, and a whole slew of other "grownboyisms." These men are so-called influencers in our society. These are major artists, entertainers, radio personalities, TV personalities and so on. These are people who others look up to because they've achieved the American Dream, so to speak. The American Dream in the mind of many is only measured by material things; not many take into account the intangibles and the things money can't buy. The American Dream has become the American Nightmare. Many don't realize it yet. The sources of influence today are oftentimes fatherless (unlearned) and they teach from their ignorance, brokenness or pain. They don't see the world for what it is; they see it for what they are. Their vantage point is a disadvantaged one and they speak from that place. The position they hold in life affords them the opportunity to convince others that this way of thinking is correct and that it must be one of the reasons why this individual has reached success. What we must remember is that some things are just given and not everything is earned. And not everything that's earned is earned the right way or for the right reasons. Satan runs the world, but does that make it right? Therefore, just because someone is in a place of power or influence doesn't mean that his or her logic is correct. Success isn't permanent, and if you watch long enough, most of the people that you deemed successful become tragedies before it's all over if their mindset wasn't in line with God's principles for living in the first place.

We must always remember that God's principles for living never changes. Just because our society's morals and values may change, God's principles remain the same. We can get away with our immorality for a period of time, but there will always be a high price to pay. I heard the saying, "Sin will take you farther than you want to go, keep you longer than you want to stay, and cost you more than you want to pay." It's very important that we keep that fact near and dear to our hearts.

IV
How the Media
Perpetuates the Cycle

Music:

Music is the most powerful form of media in our world today. The artists of today have more power than the President. It's been taught that Satan was the minister of music in Heaven. I've never read that for myself in the Bible, but it sure does make perfect sense to me because he's most influential through music. My wife and I were just talking about old school R&B and how it was comprised of more love songs than sex songs. We were listening to the 90's radio in her car and the songs that were playing were telling a story of love. They were stories of two people being completely infatuated for one another or about a man that would go to any extent to please his woman. Today's music is about instant gratification. It's about pre-marital sex, adultery, objectifying women, degrading women, using women, abusing women, and letting the man off the hook. Not only are men making music to degrade women, but women also are making music to degrade them. The artists have fallen into the "sex sells" trap and now feel that unless they try to sell sex, they won't be successful. The men are talking about how they like threesomes and so on. The women are talking about all they'll do with this "grown boy" during their one-night stand. The artists are helping make babies for whom they will not be there to help provide for. This is not to say that music of the past wasn't baby-making music, because some of it was made for that purpose. However, at least the music of our past had a balance; even if it was baby-making music, it wasn't about disrespecting a woman in the process. It was about putting her on a pedestal and appreciating her body.

Hip-hop has taken a drastic turn for the worse. I'm not a hip-hop head but even when I hear music from the 80's and 90's, there isn't much of it that has a positive message. There are about just enough mainstream artists with positive messages to count on one hand. More often than not, those artists don't last long and are forced to go back underground because the powers that be don't want to let them be a beacon of light or hope. If the artist isn't willing to be used to help destroy the minds of society, then they can't be used. Today, you'll find that even some of the most soulful music on the radio has a dark or twisted message. Hip-hop today is on a road to destruction, but who can we blame? It's hard to get mad at a 20-something year old black man who came from nothing and is now making hundreds of thousands or millions of dollars making music for a living. He's doing all he knows how and he's a product of his environment. Even if he started out with pure intentions or the grand master plan to change the world without the world ever noticing what he was doing, he quickly found out that they knew exactly what he was trying to do and they forced him to do it their way or give up all that he's earned and head back to poverty with his head hanging low. There's that group of artists who aren't quite clean enough to be Christian artists but aren't quite dirty enough to be mainstream secular artists, so they are stuck in the middle and forced to choose a side. Some fade into extinction and some make a decision that they regret for a lifetime. It's a tough space to be in for anyone. We see artists today get a chance to be who they always dreamed of being for one album, and then after that, they are forced in or forced out. I remember listening to Kanye West when he released his first album and I could feel the struggle. All of his music was hunger music and he was a starving artist just trying to eat. That was the best music of his life. Although today he's viewed as one of the greatest rappers to ever do it, a conscious-minded person couldn't listen to his music without feeling like they're blaspheming God. His music has gone from hungry to greedy. It's gone from pure to almost an abomination in many forms. It's genius what he does with a beat and his verses, but some of it is so full of blasphemy, it's like you can feel your skin burning while listening to it. I can't say that his music is part of the reason for a decline in society because most of it is so deep that the listener doesn't even know what message they are receiving. In most songs, the blasphemy or satanic references are in the scrambled chorus or the imagery in the video. The naked eye doesn't catch it or even know what they're seeing. Most get that one album and then it all shifts from there. As far as the content goes, it usually gets darker and darker or dumber and dumber. You rarely see a rapper become more conscious or cautious in their music. It really shows you what our society is reinforcing.

Somewhere along the line, it became cool to have two women at once. I'm not even sure these guys really do this or if they rap about it because it sounds cool. Nonetheless, more and more females are subjecting themselves to this treatment, thinking it'll keep their men around. It all stems from the rap music. Everybody wants to be cool like an artist. They have all the girls, they have all the money, and they have all the fame. They have what we see as *the life*, the American dream. Subconsciously, most men desire that and may not even realize that we are jealous of the rappers and are doing whatever we can in life to get closer to that level of living. We see their shine, but we don't see their struggle. We don't factor in that most of the lyrics are lies and most of the stunting they're doing is only in the music videos.

I remember when I was around the age of twenty years old and my two favorite rappers were Jeezy and

Plies. I'm from the South so they were the hottest rappers around that time. Their music resonated the most with the streets. If you'd been around drugs, sold drugs and loved women, then they were your favorite. I didn't understand then the power of music and how it affects the subconscious mind. I had no idea that the subconscious mind can't decipher between fact and fiction and that anything it receives, it accepts as a fact unless it's reversed by the conscious mind. Therefore, in the act of submissively listening to music and letting it speak to me, I was, in fact, under the spell of that music. That music began to shape my outlook on life, my attitude about myself, the world, and the women around me. I subconsciously moved closer to the messages in that music. During that time, I was selling drugs to get ahead in life. I was carrying a gun with me everywhere I went. I quit my job and started selling drugs. I was in college but I wasn't paying attention in class. I'd go to class with an empty folder and a small backpack. That backpack had a quarter pound of marijuana in it and a .380 handgun. I carried those two things daily. I'd leave class early to make a sale. I'd stay up until 4 am either making sells or breaking down the weed into five and ten dollar bags. The rappers confirmed in their music what I grew up seeing my cousins and friends doing all my life. If you sell drugs, you make fast money, get a lot of women, and get a lot of respect. That was the mindset and the message being passed down. Although these rappers lived in huge houses and drove a lot of cars all from legal money, they never said that in a song. The rappers had one lady and maybe cheated from time to time, but they never said that in a song. Well, at least not in their hits. Plies had been a college football player just as I'd been for three years. I never heard him say that in a song. Plies had a college education. That was something that I didn't have and something that I never did get. He had accomplished things in his life that his music discouraged me from pursuing. The places where his music was leading me, he'd never been; the prison or the grave. I'm naming him as an example but I'm not blaming him. I'm simply stating a fact and using a real-life example so that you understand that this really happens. Most people may never realize what's happening to them or they may lack the maturity to admit that it did in fact happen to them. Many say that "its just music," but I'm here to tell you that it's much more than music. Music becomes a blueprint for life. Music is the most powerful form of media because it heads directly to the subconscious mind. I know that for a fact now because I was a willing participant in the misleading power of music. I was led to believe that this lifestyle was what would gain my stripes as a man. I was living alone and trying to find a way in the world as a man. I didn't want to reach out to my parents because I was a grown man, so I watched and listened to see how some other men made it. I figured that selling drugs or being a goon was a rite of passage and that somehow, that would lead me down a path to manhood.

I was not only selling drugs and carrying a gun to school, but I also started a somewhat organized pimping operation. I became a dealer in women both for myself and also for other men. I manipulated women and used my looks, demeanor and way with words to persuade women to do things out of their character. It ranged from dancing near naked in a club to sleeping with 2-5 men in the same night. Most of the women did it for free. You see, what happened here was the result of being victims of a fatherless society. We didn't have enough positive male role models to look up to and emulate. Some of us had fathers, but each of them was only one man--outside of them—we were bombarded with negative imagery from all angles. Even the best of fathers would have had the fight of his life trying to keep his kids from the lure of the hip-hop world. I was influenced to sell drugs, carry a gun and manipulate women. The women were being influenced by the same things that influenced me, so they gave into it willingly. The women thought it would make them sexy, attractive and desirable if they sold their bodies or gave their bodies away. They thought that the shorter their skirts, the better off they would appear in the eyes of men. The young ladies I manipulated didn't know that what they were doing could affect their lives and self-esteem forever. They had no clue that it could cost them their husbands one day. We were all in a trap. We were all misled. We were all living a lie. This is what happens in a fatherless society.

We can't just blame the music because we must realize that those making the music are also victims of this fatherless society. We want them to accept responsibility and do better, but they don't know better in order to do better. The artist is simply trying to eat, and when you're hungry, you'll do anything. The orders are coming from higher up. His conscience kicks in at some point and even though he tries to put it out for the public, he is forced to shelve it or change it to something more secular and reckless. If he bucks the system, then he will once again be an independent artist. It's difficult to go from making hundreds of thousands or millions of dollars to be being broke again just because you want to make music with a positive message. So he convinces himself that he will just play the game by the industry's rules just long enough to get a platform where he can call the shots. Then one day, he wakes up and realizes that will never be the case. The journey to the top is so long that by the time he arrives, he has become who he was being forced to be. He has forgotten who he once was or the person he wanted to be.

Is it fair for us to ask this young man who started with nothing to give up all he has and make positive music that maybe he wouldn't even understand himself? Or do we sit back and let him continue to be a product of this fatherless society and just accept it for what it is? The buck has to stop somewhere. The messages have to be broken down somewhere. Someone has to take a stand and make a change. The world will self-destruct and no one will care; or will it just be those who are part of the hip-hop generation who kill themselves off and rid the world of its problems? If you sit back and look at it, you have to ask yourself, is that the grand master plan?

Record label: Why do you reject an artist's music with a positive and wholesome message but then promote his destructive music like there is no tomorrow? Why do you ignore the black men killing black men everyday because of a hip-hop battle or gang mentality that's perpetuated in the rappers' music? Why do you ignore the teen pregnancies that are at an all-time high because of the R&B sex lessons the artists are putting out? Why do you ignore the pain and the vicious cycle that your music is perpetuating? Oh, I know! That's not your problem is it? Maybe it will be your problem when your daughter is pregnant at 16. Maybe it will be your problem when your son is sagging his pants, smoking weed and popping mollies. Maybe it will be your problem when your child threatens to commit suicide after listening to Rihanna's "Russian Roulette" song one too many times. Maybe it will be your problem then.

Someone has to do something, but we can't expect the masses to take action. It starts at home. Mothers and fathers must tighten the boundaries on their kids and lay down the law. Today, you must do more talking than you've ever done. You have to get into your child's subconscious and conscious mind just as the music does. Listen to the music they're listening to and combat those messages with truth, wisdom and understanding. Make this your problem before it becomes your problem.

How TV affects us:

I've been reading lately about new reality shows being released and even some being cancelled. One show that was promoting the lifestyle of a rapper with 11 "baby mommas" was recently cancelled because one individual decided to stand up and fight. She took on an entire network and she won. Once again, this show would have been a part of the hip-hop movement today. This woman decided that enough was enough, and she started making calls to the president of the network and demanding that the show be dropped. She followed that with action and started a petition on which she received over 20,000 signatures. She made a lot of noise. She appeared on the news, in blogs, and so on. The network pulled the show from its lineup. I know that was a blow to the cast of the show, but it's what needed to happen for our society's sake. That show would have only hurt the black community, making it even more laughable. Viewers of other races would have sat back scratching their heads in confusion while laughing in amusement. The black race would have taken another huge blow and come closer to being out for the count.

There are several other shows that diminish the quality of television today and this issue spans across all races. It's not just a black thing when it comes to TV. It's a "people" thing. We have shows that are called "housewives" but they are mostly comprised of house-girlfriends. We have shows where the women are called "wives" but they are mostly comprised of ex-girlfriends, baby mommas, and so on. So what's happening is the media is passing these women off as wives when 90% of them aren't. The young girls watching these shows in their bedrooms while their parents are asleep are being taught that it is perfectly okay to be a live-in girlfriend and have a man's child as long as he buys you a nice car and nice clothes. It's okay to be cheated on and occasionally cursed out and beat on as long as you have a nice car and some clothes. Then with all your hurt and anger, go out into the world and take it out on other women. Hate on them and make them hate you because deep down, they are just jealous that they aren't you. That's the message that the TV shows of today are sending, a message that the casts on the shows either don't realize it or don't care. After all, they have to eat, too. It comes down to the survival tactics. We live in a world of surviving, not thriving. We are just trying to get by. If I have to kill you off so that I can eat, then that's what I'm going to do. That's what we are subconsciously taught in our society. If I have to run your life in the ground and influence you to ruin your life so that my TV show can have ratings, then that's what I'm going to do.

Screw you and the mother you came out of, oh and the God that made you. God didn't make junk, but I'm going to turn you into junk. That's the message that a lot of media is sending us.

Now when I write it the way I just wrote it, does it strike you a bit differently than what you thought you were watching on TV? You see, that's how your subconscious mind picks up the message and decodes it. Your subconscious mind can decode anything and begin to move towards it as if it's God's law for your life, and you may never even realize that you're headed that way. There's too much power in the human mind. In order to combat those messages, you must be aware of what you're watching. I always say that we must guard our eyes and our ears because those are the quickest routes to our minds.

If you don't believe me, just watch. If your lady surfs on Instagram or watches reality TV every week, watch and see how she begins to change. Watch her try to pick petty arguments and start checking your phone, Twitter and Facebook account every day, questioning you about every move. Watch her start to drop hints and throw subliminal messages about all the other girls' new purses, cars and so on. Watch her birthday list and Christmas list begin to change. You'll notice that she once was very happy with a Coach purse, but now all she wants is Louis Vuitton. She once loved Chili's, but now she can't stand anything less than a $50 plate. Why is she changing like that? It's her input. Your income hasn't changed. You haven't changed your taste, but why has hers changed? Well, her favorite programs show all these reality TV stars pulling up in Range Rovers. They all eat at the nicest restaurants and they all carry Louis Vuitton purses. Truthfully, the men in their lives bought most of these material items. If not, then most of it is rented, borrowed or leased. A year or so after the show ends, most of these reality TV stars lose the lifestyles that they had during the taping of the shows because they never knew how to maintain what they had and only wanted it to look grander than it really was. I'm not being harsh; I'm being real. I'm just telling the truth. Yes, there is a minority group of those who own their material possessions and bought everything with their own money, but they are far and few between. In addition, those who truthfully bought their homes, cars and fine things with their own money practically used blood money because of all the minds they ruined to earn those platforms and that money. Can we blame them? No, we can't. Can we be mad at them? No, we can't. They are simply trying to eat. They are simply trying to survive. They are simply trying to feed their kids. The change starts with you. The change starts in your home. Stop allowing those TV shows to play on your television. Go into every room in your house and put a block on those channels. Fellas, stop desiring women who watch those shows. Let that question be in your Rolodex of inquiries on your first date. You must also make sure that you are her equal. You can't ask her not to watch junk TV if you're listening to junk music. The rap music will affect your mindset just as much as the TV will affect hers. A change must come.

Don't get me wrong; I'm not mad at the reality stars. I don't believe it's their intention to go on television and ruin minds. I don't think they thought it would come to that at all. Most of them thought they would just be on TV talking about and showing their lives. They didn't know they'd be set up like rats in a cage, antagonized, and forced to fight like animals or idiots. They didn't know that the "reality" of their lives would be diced and chopped on the editing floor. They were not aware that only half of their sentences would be aired and not the other half that fully explains what they were trying to say. They didn't know that the antecedent of their behavior would be cut out but their behavior would be displayed in slow motion so that they could be made villains and buffoons. They didn't know they would be despised in the public eye and shrunk down to the equivalent of cartoon entertainment. I'm just quoting what viewers say about the show. I don't actually watch the shows myself on a regular basis. I have seen them all at least once, and once was enough for me. I see their ignorance of the world they've entered. I see their innocence like a herd of sheep being led to the slaughter. I see it in their eyes. I see it in their actions. I see it in their pain and frustration after the show airs and they are despised and ripped apart by every critic in America. They are forced to cling onto the praises of teenage girls who don't have fathers at home or know any better. They are forced to cling onto the praises of "frienemies" who secretly despise them and are waiting for their fall. They are forced to cling onto the praises of the fake or feeble-minded because they just want to be loved. They want to be significant. They want to matter just like every other human being. It's not in their hearts to tear down society. That wasn't the goal when they signed their first contract to appear on TV for very little money. They saw it as fun, as an opportunity to gain a platform and a following. Very few have managed to make it out more successful than they were prior to being cast. Very few have really capitalized from a reality show. The rest kind of fade into the obscurity of insignificance out of shame or due to the cold world turning its back on them. They realize that fifteen minutes of fame wasn't worth a lifetime of misery and regret. My prayer is that these shows won't affect them forever. My prayer is that they do not lose themselves in the search for significance. My prayer is that the results will not be the same for me when I'm given the same opportunity. That is why I can't judge them; I understand that they are just pawns on a chessboard in a game that they didn't even realize they were playing. They are a part of a grand master plan that's bigger than them.

It is Satan's plan to slowly and miserably ruin God's world and His children. I know that sounds spooky but that's what it is. We aren't fighting a physical battle; this is spiritual warfare. I won't go much deeper into that because my point will be lost.

We have to stand up and fight the battles we feel are necessary. If it hits too close to home, then do something about it. Like the lady who singlehandedly shut down a TV show she found to be disgraceful. She wasn't playing any games and she accomplished what she set out to do. Not every network will care. Not every network will listen, especially when the people at large are still tuning in to the nonsense. You can't change the world but you can change yourself. You can change your household and your change just might spark someone else's change. I have been fortunate enough to meet and speak with a lot of reality stars and even some producers of some of these despicable shows. For the ones that will listen, I take the time to speak into their lives. I show them the mirror of their actions. I talk to them about what's really happening and how their roles in this are affecting the world. Some take heed and start to slowly make changes. The others will have to learn the hard way when the consequences hit home so hard that they can't ignore it any longer. I'm doing all I can to prevent it. Maybe the head of a network or a top producer will read this part of my book and feel compelled to give me an opportunity to produce positive television and start a movement. No one knows what God has in store for those who seek change. You have to want it and you have to be willing to do something about it.

I recall two things recently that came to my desk from individuals who had seen the effects of reality TV right in front of their eyes. One was a young lady who told me about elementary school girls screaming at each other and pointing in one another's faces while using the curse words and terminology that had become famous on a particular reality show. She was shocked and appalled by the influence that these shows had on even these little girls. All she could do was shake her head and shed a tear. Now she had to go in and break up this fight and try to explain to these young souls why this behavior is not acceptable or cute in any way. It's hard trying to rewire the mind after it's been imprinted with so many negative messages. Yes, this should have been stopped at home, but when it isn't and you see it, be man enough to speak up and say something about it. Speak into your child's life daily. Speak into the lives of other children daily. Don't ever sit by and watch something play out and just shake your head. Speak up and be a voice. Be a light in this dark world. You never know what you may utter to an impressionable child that could change his life.

After that incident, I received a call from a young man who had watched his girlfriend change. He had been with her for years and even had a child with her, but all of a sudden within the course of a couple years, with reality TV and other toxic shows being on the rise, she began to change. These TV programs became her favorite shows and influenced her in a negative way. The relationship was no longer about love. It became about money. If money couldn't buy love, then she didn't want it. He made good money and could afford some nice things, but she wanted more. She didn't want the things he'd buy for her; she wanted the things she saw on her favorite reality shows. She wanted a glamorous lifestyle like the reality stars, even if those people on TV didn't truthfully have lives as dazzling as they made it seem. She wanted that, but he didn't want that for his life. He couldn't put up with it much longer. He dreamed of having money to spare and not spending every dime to keep up with the crowd. He dreamed of growing old with a savings and retirement fund instead of being in debt and maxed out on credit cards. What she wanted for life, he wanted no parts of it. He tried to talk to her, he tried to change her and he tried to convince her that she was chasing vanity. She never got the message, and he had to make a choice for his life. He decided to break it off with her and move on with his life; now, he's forced to love his child from a distance. He couldn't sit by idly and condone this behavior. He knew that it would be his finances that made the lifestyle possible, and he knew that if he gave in, it could ruin his soon-to-be-wife and his child for good. He couldn't do it.

You see, our media and the things we put into our minds can ruin our lives. It can ruin us as individuals and it can also ruin our families. We must realize before it's too late when we are being sucked into the trap of this fatherless society.

V
What is a Real Man?

Almost nothing that we've learned about being a real man is actually part of being a man, unless you've learned it directly from a real man. I've had guys tell me that they learned what it is to be a man from TV shows or music. One guy told me he learned how to treat women from movies he watched growing up with his older brothers. A single mom raised him so the only lessons on manhood he received were from television. After hearing that, I knew he would have a world full of wakeup calls when he actually found his wife and would have to live with her everyday. It was an honest truth that so many other men find relatable. He told me that when he'd meet women or spend the night with a woman, he would do the things he saw on a movie, like the time Eddie Murphy was in bed with a woman in a movie and pulled up the covers to see what her feet looked like. Because of that image in his mind, feet became an issue with every woman he met. He'd analyze her hands and feet and then went from there. It wasn't about her character, her mind, her goals, and so on. It was about the superficial things first and then the intangibles were a plus. That's how we are conditioned as men in our society. We are trained by music and television to determine what a man is, what a man does, and what he looks for in a woman. Ninety-nine percent of it is garbage, but unless we don't have those messages refuted, then we live out the rest of our lives believing them.

At the core of a real man is the ability to accept responsibility. The likes and dislikes of a man and all the small things that can change from man to man have no bearings on manhood. Accepting responsibility is the number one thing that the world needs most. A real man is responsible for himself and for his family. A real man is responsible for the choices he makes in life and he takes responsibility for the knowledge he's to seek out in life to better provide for himself and his family. At the core of a man, that is what matters most.

I am a real man today because I've accepted responsibility for my life and for my family. I love my wife. I'm FAITFHFUL to my wife. I provide for my wife. I love my kids. I'm faithful to my kids. I provide for my kids. I don't have a college degree, but I'm not blaming my parents for that. I'm not blaming the rappers for that. I'm not blaming the white man for that. I'm not blaming God for that. I'm not blaming myself for that. Instead I accepted responsibility for myself and took the steps to get the knowledge I needed to provide for my family. In total, I got formal education for 21 years of my life. Then I accepted responsibility and began getting self-education. Within two years, I found financial freedom and got on a path to making more money than the salary I would have earned with the degree I was seeking in college. I'm not knocking college or the idea of acquiring an education. What I'm saying is that I accepted responsibility for my life and did what I needed to do in order to learn and grow so that I could provide for my family and myself.

I grew to realize that everything affects everything. I realized that my actions would affect my wife and my children. If my actions were positive and purpose-driven, then it would have a positive effect on their lives. If my actions were negative and selfishly driven, then it would have a negative effect on their lives. If I would have continued to sell drugs after I got married, then my wife would have left for good and I wouldn't have been a factor in my son's life. Instead, I started learning, growing and striving to be like Christ. My wife fell in love with me all over again, my son fell in love with me and I strengthened our family. If I would have fallen in love with the strip clubs, the club, or hanging out with the boys, it would have driven a wedge between my wife and me. I would have tempted myself enough to start several affairs. I would have lost my wife's trust and broken her heart. I would have lost my son's trust and broken his heart. I would have inadvertently taught my son that men run from their responsibilities and live their lives on their own terms. I would have taught my son that it's perfectly acceptable to upset the mother of his child, cause her to leave him and then take care of his children only on the weekends or not at all. Everything affects everything. Instead of continuing to make bad choices, I accepted responsibility and made the right choices. I could have quit my job before I found my purpose and forced my wife to work her fingers to the bone to provide for my son and me. What would that have taught my son? It would have taught him that men take shortcuts in life that result in their women taking care of them when they don't want to take care of themselves. So many men are teaching that lesson to their children by quitting their jobs and chasing fantasies because they don't want to work for "the man," and then their families pay the price for it and end up in poverty. I realized that I must do what I *had* to do so that one day, I could do what I *wanted* to do. I sacrificed and I worked a job that I hated until I found a surefire way to walk away from the job and never look back. Now I stand on a platform that allows me to write a book and earn double in nine months of what I was making on my past job in a whole year. What would have happened if I'd quit my job back when I did not profit from my first book? What would have happened if I had given into my ego, left my job and told "the man" to shove his job somewhere? This was back when I received my royalty check for only $300 for 3 whole months of book sales! How would I have been able to face my wife and son?

Many men are doing that to their families today. They are being selfish and doing what they want to do rather than what they need to do. Being a man is about accepting responsibility for your actions and the consequences that come with them. With every action, there is an equal or greater reaction. As a man, you must be willing to accept that and make the best choices to set your family up for the future. It's a never-ending battle.

Raise Your Kids:

As men, it's important that we raise our own kids. If the woman isn't worth marrying, then she's not worth impregnating. Stop sticking your thing in a woman you wouldn't marry. If you're doing that, then you are not being a man; you are being a boy. You are making an action but are not willing to accept the consequences that come with that action. That's what "grown boys" do, not what grown men do. I understand that you may have already done that. I understand that you may have done it more than once, but it's never too late to become a man. Start today and make better choices from this point forward. Start looking for a wife so that you can start a real family and raise your kids.

For the kids who don't live with you, make sure you call them everyday. That's the least you can do. You may not have money to give them and you may not have all the time in the world to give them, but call your kids daily and tell them you love them. Teach them a daily lesson about life, even if it's the same one. I have an uncle who would tell me every time I saw him that "winners never quit and quitters never win." My uncle is over 50 years old now and serving a 35-year prison sentence, but I'll never forget those words he spoke into my life every time I saw him. Guess what? I'm not quitting and I'm winning. The message had an impact on my life even though it was a delayed one. He wasn't able to make that phrase work in his life yet, but somehow it worked in mine. I'm hopeful that one day those words will work in my uncle's life as well. The lesson behind that is that you may not be perfect and you may not be able to set the example for every lesson you give your kids, but teach it to them anyway. You never know how their lives will manifest because of something you taught them while they were growing up. Kids have a way of holding onto something all of their lives, so be very careful what you deposit into your children. Read this book twice, call me and set up a coaching session, learn all that you can learn and then teach. Make sure that you have dealt with your own demons so you don't pass those down to your kids. Look yourself in the mirror and declare to become a man, and then take massive action before you pass anything negative down to your kids. So often, we hurt and we pass that hurt down to our kids. We perpetuate the cycle and we keep the domino effect going. It's time to man up. It's time to grow up. It's time to become a better man. It's time to do something that you've never done so that you can have something that you've never had. We need real men in our world.

When men accept responsibility for our lives, then our world begins to change. I don't just mean our interpersonal world; I mean our entire world. The world we live in begins to change. How does it do that? When we as men accept responsibility, then the men around us begin to do the same because no man wants another man to be anymore of a man than him. We create a positive effect in the world when we accept responsibility. Our wives will grow to love us even more and that will help us heal from our past hurts and love ourselves even more. It will strengthen our marriages, and when our marriages are strengthened, we love our kids better. We teach our kids better. We teach them not only with words but also with our actions. Our children grow up to emulate us and pass that down to their kids, and the cycle continues. This is how we change our world when we change ourselves.

Look over your life and ask yourself what you can start doing on a daily basis to become a better man. You can read your Bible everyday. You can learn something everyday. You can do something for your wife that she can do for herself. You can spend time with your kids every day, whether it's in person or on the phone. If you can't reach your kids because their mother hates you, then you can start to rebuild that relationship. You can send her flowers every week. You can send her a nice text message everyday asking for forgiveness. I promise you that she will forgive you. She will let you be a father to your child if you show that you are man enough to be a good father. If you're too arrogant, childish and bitter to apologize to the woman who you lied to and misled, then how can she trust you to be a good example to your child? If you're too arrogant or childish to forgive her for the pain she caused you, then how can she trust you to not pass that pain and anger down to your child? The best thing you can do for your children is to love their mother. That doesn't mean you have to be with her if you know that's not an option, but it does mean you need to treat her like a lady and respect her so that you can show your child how a woman should be treated and respected. Be transparent with your kids. The best parents are transparent. Teach your kids from your mistakes. Open up about your immaturity and the mistakes you made as a man so that they don't make the same mistakes. Teach your kids how to live and succeed in life. You do not have to reside in the home to be present in your child's life. Don't let your past mistakes create a permanent situation. Work on your past mistakes and make them right so that you can have an impact in your child's life. Your child needs you! If you are unwilling to be in your child's life by any means necessary, then you are unwilling to be a man and you are unfit to lead in any aspect of life. You do not deserve a wife, and any kind of blessings. And you won't receive them either. If you do not want to accept responsibility in this aspect of your life, then you do not deserve responsibility in any aspect of your life. Confront yourself as a man today. If you have to cry, then cry. If you have to scream, then scream. If you need to call your dad, then call your dad. If you need to call me, then call me. Do what you need to do in order to be a man. It's time for you to stop running and stop making excuses. It's time to accept responsibility for your life and be a real man. The world needs you. Your kids need you. Your wife needs you.

A real man accepts responsibility. The time is now! BE A MAN!!!

VI
Embracing Emotions

I'm not sure if we will ever get this part right. It has been engrained in us from the beginning of time in such a fashion that I wonder if we will ever be able to reverse it. It's a very tricky subject because although we want to be able to embrace our emotions, we don't want men to be identical to women in this department. God made us different for a reason. What we have to do here is understand those differences and embrace who we are instead of trying to be who we think we're supposed to be. What I mean is that God also made men in such a way that we could cry too. We may not cry as easily as women, but we also have tear glands and when we feel the need, we should use them. We have emotions just like women do and we feel them the same, but because of the way society has shaped us, we fight them. We don't embrace them; we try to elude them. This creates a negative effect in our bodies and our minds. Emotions are vital to human life and they all work in ways to keep the cycle of the mind and body in harmony. When we sneeze, we must close our eyes. You've never sneezed once without your eyes closing. You may not know why that happens, but you know it happens. We must vent, cry, and express for the same reasons. Our bodies are designed to do those things. We need to release those emotions so that we can start over fresh and new. What does too much pressure do if it builds up inside of anything? It bursts. The same happens with us as men. When we hold back our tears, our thoughts, and our emotions, one day we burst. That combustion may hurt or even kill someone. In most cases, it just hurts someone and usually, it's the woman in our lives. The combustion gives us a release. It feels good to us, and it hurts her. Maybe it was cursing her out. Maybe it was hitting her. Maybe it was threatening her. Whatever it was, it felt good in that moment because you were releasing pressure. The only problem is that if you had been releasing pressure over the course of your life, those small emissions wouldn't have hurt anyone because they would have been in the form of a heartfelt conversation or a few tears. Instead, you have held it in for years and now it's become anger and rage, and when you combust, you release violence. It hurts somebody and then it trickles down to others. Some men hurt their women, which in turn, hurts their children. Sometimes the hurt trickles down to the woman's parents, causing them to wonder where they went wrong raising their daughter. In actuality, the parents didn't do anything wrong raising their daughter. It was the man that broke their daughter. The cycle goes on and on. It's been passed down that men can't cry. Men can't hurt publicly. Men can't express too much emotion, say too much, or give too much of themselves. This rationale sets us up for failure, and we end up hurting our loved ones and ourselves, and no one realizes the root of this problem.

Now is the time to change that. It's time that men begin to express themselves little by little. If you need to cry, then cry. When you're hurt by your woman, then sit down and tell her. When you're hurting from something your mother or father did, then sit down and tell them. Cry with it if you need to. If they aren't around for you to tell them, then hire a therapist. Get it off of your chest. Don't let that pain, frustration and confusion sit on your chest because one day, it will burst and it will cost you greatly.

I remember growing up and being a crybaby at a very young age. I was very emotional and I would cry about everything. My parents didn't stop me from crying or tell me to "man up" and stop crying. They also didn't instruct me to express why I was crying. I didn't know why I was crying half the time. It could have been because I was babied or spoiled as an infant and toddler and it just grew with me and caused me to cry whenever something didn't go my way. I'm not sure why I was that way. Another thing was that I never wrestled with my dad or play fought, nor did I do that with friends. I believe that kept me soft. I grew up very shy, quiet and passive. I have an inner strength that allowed me to say no to peer pressure and excel in sports, but outside of that, I was very passive. I would get pushed and just walk away. If someone threatened to beat me up, I wouldn't say a word back. I never got hit without hitting back, and I never got into a fight that I lost, but I just wasn't the typical guy when it came to aggression. I played football and I was always the best running back because I enjoyed running for my life. You couldn't catch me to save your life because I was running to save mine. I'd score almost four touchdowns a game and average over 10 yards a carry. I averaged over 10 yards a carry in high school as well. If I was put on defense, you couldn't pay me to lay someone out. When I was young playing in the city league, I'd strategically run to the side of the guy and let him pass me, and then I'd run him down from behind. I was always the fastest guy in the league and I could run anyone down, but I'd never hit them head on. That said a lot about my personality and I have no earthly idea why I was like that. I had just never been introduced to contact like most guys. Most guys have an older brother, cousin or someone who roughs them up. I didn't have that. All of my cousins were girls and my male cousins were into other stuff like their own girls or running the streets with their older friends and getting into trouble. So here I was a complete heterosexual male but forced to play with all girls, so we played things like "house." Man, writing this really makes me cringe, but hey, I'm leading by example and expressing emotion. Occasionally while growing up, I'd play "throw 'em up, bust 'em up" with my friends. I was always good at that because no one could catch me to tackle me, and I would strategically never have the right angle to tackle anyone running at me with the ball. Man, I was soft. I grew to the point where I stopped crying because I knew it was frowned upon in our society. So, I began to bottle everything up on the inside. I began to harbor anger and resentment. I observed everything, and I decoded it in my own my mind without asking any questions as to why things were that way. It shaped the way I thought and the things I did. After I left home at 18 to go to college on a full scholarship, I began to search for myself as a man. I had all these years of downloaded information that most likely had all been misperceived on my part. I thought I knew what a man was, but I really had no idea.

I walked around frowning all the time. I literally had a frown on my face. Not just a blank, expressionless face, but a real frown like I was angry at the world. I was trying to be a man. I was trying to be tough in this cold world. I wanted to be and feel like I'd never been and felt before. No, please don't let your mind wander too far. I'm not gay, never was, never thought about it, and never will be. I'm 100% a heterosexual man. I just wasn't aggressive, assertive or expressive. I was quiet, solemn, and serious nearly all the time. I would loosen up around close guy friends and clown around, but I never showed a weak or sensitive side to a woman. If I did cry in front of a woman, it was to gain her sympathy so that I could play on it later. I became a liar, a manipulator, a thief, a criminal and a hater. I was everything negative and not much positive, and it was all because I never embraced emotions. I let it all build up, and it made me evil. Now that I'm healed, I look around and see men who are just like my former self. It hurts to see it, and hopefully this book will give many men freedom from that pain and confusion.

I kept holding in my pain and frustration, and then I began to explode. It happened in a relationship in college. I was young and immature and had no idea what it meant to be a man. My girlfriend at the time had no idea what a man was either. Her dad had been abusive to her mom, her sisters' boyfriends were abusive to them, and her only brother was in prison. She was clueless as to what a real man was too, so she was just open to accepting what ever she got. In fact, she was inclined to have a man who was closest to what she'd always known. In her mind, if a man didn't abuse her, he didn't love her. In her mind, love was pain. I remember her saying; "I love it when you're mad." She wanted to be controlled and told what to do. It made her think I was more of a man if I did those things. A loving, caring, understanding man that let her do what she wanted to do would have been considered a pushover. She wanted a man who would be assertive and put his foot down. She had no clue what she was asking for. At first, it starts out cute and cuddly, but then it escalates into violence. She and I were a very bad mix. Here you have two young adults that had no idea about real love, a real relationship, and what a real man and woman look like. We had both received visuals in our lives that we accepted as normalcy, and we never learned otherwise. Me, being a confused young man full of pain and rage, and her, being a naïve young lady full or ignorance and bliss, we were a disaster waiting to happen. After about a year of me trying to control and change her, all the emotion that built up all my life began to surface, and I exploded. The relationship turned violent. There was pushing and pulling, screaming and yelling. For some of you reading this, you may have lived this reality yourselves, or at least have seen it. For those of you reading this that haven't experienced it, don't feel untouchable or invincible. Abuse has no face and does not care who you are. If there is a combustible mixture of emotions inside of you, it can be triggered and brought out of you. This violence would happen, then I'd break down and cry, and then she'd break down and forgive me. She'd go shower and come out and ask to have sex with me. How twisted could we be? Yes, that was real, and I know that I am not the only one who has lived it. This was a combination of a man who never expressed himself and a woman who didn't know what a man really was. Our worlds collided, and we almost ruined one another. We were toxic and bad for one another. You see, I can speak on so much because I've been through the worst. I am not sitting on a high horse looking down on you and pointing the finger. I'm trying to pull you up to higher ground. I have been at the bottom of the misconceptions of manhood. Now I'm at the top with the reality of what truly makes someone a man.

I honestly believe that had I embraced my emotions and expressed my heart, my mind, my feelings, my thoughts, my worries, and my fears, then I could have avoided a lot of this pain. I could have avoided that combustion, myself some heartache and could have done the same for that young woman. I finally got it together and decided that I wanted better for my life. I did not want to be a man who had to scare a woman into submission. I did not want to be a man who had to beat a woman into submission. I did not want to be a man who had to lie, deceive, or coerce a woman to love me. I wanted to be loved for being a good man, a real man. I wanted better for myself, and I wanted better for her. In pain and in frustration, I ended that relationship and I moved on. I ended up returning to her for six months, but then I moved on again for good. We both needed better in life. We both needed something new and a chance to learn real love and to grow. I moved on in attempts to become a real man. I met my wife next, and with her, I became a man. She knew differently than my ex because she had seen her mother live a life full of strength. She had received her own visuals and decoded them herself. What she gathered was that a woman is not a footstool or a do-girl. A woman is to be submissive, but only to a man who understands his mission in life. A woman must stand her ground and love herself in order to truly be loved by a man. She stuck to those things, and it made me a better man. Today, I'm able to cry to my wife if I need to. When my feelings are hurt, I can tell her how and why they are hurting. When I'm upset about something or want something to change, I can express those things to her and we make those changes together. I no longer harbor negative emotions, anger, hurt and pain. I release my emotions as they come and I express myself, as I need to. It has strengthened me as a man. I have become a real man full of confidence. I no longer fear life. I no longer fear any other human being. I'm not afraid to fight anymore if I have to. Of course I don't want to, but if I had to, I'd knock a man out in confidence and not in fear or rage. I know that's not the Christian thing to do, but I'm just expressing the truth because I promised you when I told you to buy this book that it would be the realest book you've ever read. So to reiterate, I am trying to be Christ-like, but I am not Christ. I am no longer full of rage and anger. I no longer walk around trying to look or sound tough. I no longer try to look intimidating. It was always pretty impossible to do that anyway, being a black man with hazel eyes. The tough guy look just never worked for me.

I can honestly tell you that it's okay to embrace your emotions. Express yourself as you need to, and do it in love. I'm not saying yell, curse, and fight. I'm saying to sit down with the person like a man should and tell this person what's on your mind. Get it off your chest and soon as it lands there so that you don't explode after it's built up. I know so many men who see something they hate going on in their homes, and they don't say a word. Then all of a sudden one day, he's caught in an affair, or he explodes and hits or leaves his wife. Why does he do this? Because he never learned how to express himself, he let the pain build up and cause him to take actions he never really wanted to commit.

Express yourself! Open up and tell it how you feel it. Be real about your pain, your fears, your worries, your hopes and your dreams. It will do a lot more for you if you're willing to be open about your emotions. HEmotions. Embrace emotions.

VII
The Effects on Our Women

Most men can't begin to fathom the effects our lack of responsibility have on our women. From childhood, young girls are in desperate need of positive male figures in their lives just as much as a man. In a lot of cases, a young girl needs that male figure more than a young boy does. That little girl is a victim of mishaps from the time she exits the womb. As she grows, her body begins to fill out and change. She may begin to form breasts, her hips may begin to spread, her butt may begin to round and all of a sudden, she becomes an "object" in the minds of young boys, and sometimes, even grown men. Here you have this young girl without a protector in this world, if she doesn't have a responsible father or male figure in her life. She's in the world naked and vulnerable. I can't count how many women I've spoken to over the years that were molested or raped in their life. I married one. It happened to my little sister as well. That's how close to home this is for me.

Our women are prey in our society because we have become weak and ruthless men acting out of fear and pain. Our women are not safe in their own homes or around their own family because of the mindset that is being passed down amongst men. Rape happens to young girls, and oftentimes, their own mothers won't believe that it's true because the mother's new boyfriend is the perpetrator. The mother is hurting, lost, and confused because of the absence of a real man in her life so she neglects her own child to hold onto a man. Some mothers have even sacrificed their own daughters to please a "grown boy" living in their homes. Many women will do next to anything to keep a man around. I hope this is beginning to paint a picture of how desperately a positive male figure is essential to our world.

Usually, these young girls later become promiscuous after being raped or molested. Their minds are opened up to a new idea of what life is like and their bodies are introduced to this new feeling that they subconsciously could begin to crave out of a desire for closeness with a male. Many young girls are harmed beyond repair and are unable to bear children later in life. Many young girls are actually forced to become mothers while still children themselves. This is happening everyday in our society. I have met young ladies that became victims early on in life and remained victims well into adulthood. They sell their bodies or give their bodies away, hoping that it will be reciprocated with genuine love. In the process, they suffer emotional, verbal and physical abuse at the hands of a "grown boy." The woman ends up aged, with kids and still without real love. This can affect a woman in a negative way. While some women just lie down and accept this as the way of life, others find something inside of them and begin to play the game by the man's rules. This is what many call "thinking like a man." This woman begins to carry herself the same way the men in her life carry themselves. The tragedy of it all is that these aren't men. They are "grown boys." This woman starts to sleep with as many men as possible with the mindset that she's getting even or playing the game better than the man. She begins to manipulate, deceive and mentally abuse men to get what she wants. She elevates to a higher level of the game, and she plays it better than most men play it. When she slips up and gets caught, she pays the price at the end of his fists. If she lives to play the game again, she gets even craftier and vows not to make those same mistakes. Throughout this process, she's degrading her body and losing the very essence of who she was intended to be by God. She becomes a shell of herself, doing what she feels she has to do to survive. By the age of thirty, this woman has had 50 or more sexual partners, and most of them unprotected. She's been raped, molested and abused. She has either stripped for money or had sex for money. She gets up every day to do it all over again, and most nights, goes to bed not even being able to remember who she is anymore. These are the effects our "grown boy" ways have on our women.

These women are growing at the same rate as our "grown boys." In this fatherless society, the more "grown boys" that surge to a level of influence, the more women without identify surface. The young men have been denied the necessary tools to become real men and out of pain and fear, they strip the rights away from an innocent woman so that she can't become a whole woman either. Hurt people hurt people. Because the man is physically stronger with his words and with his body, he typically wins this battle. The woman is created to be submissive and loving to her partner, but because this grown boy was not raised to be a man, he doesn't appreciate those traits in a woman and ends up abusing them. He abuses her and misuses her. Instead of him letting her build him up and make him better, he makes her worse, and in turn, it makes him worse. She can't complete him because he's depleting her due to his own emptiness. This is the cycle we're in. She can't get out because her identity has been stripped. She no longer knows who she is or what she's worth. She's willing to be bought because she was never told that she was priceless. She's willing to be chained to this man's hip because she was never told that love is freedom, not captivity. She gives up everything trying to keep him. He takes everything trying not to lose himself. This is the cycle we're in.

Today, a lot of our young women degrade themselves subconsciously, hoping that if they do it to themselves, then a man won't do it to them. To her, it feels better to hurt herself than to have a man hurt her. Unfortunately, she finds out that hurting herself will not stop a "grown boy" from hurting her and that in fact, it causes him hurt her even more. She lies down with the hopes that he will pick her up. She falls in love with the hopes that he will catch her. She finds out that when she lies down, the "grown boy" mentality will run her over and let her hit rock bottom when she decides to fall in love. Oftentimes, he doesn't even know what he's doing to her because he's hurting so bad he just wants someone to feel his pain. He's so lost and confused that his survival tactics kick in and he almost destroys her literally and figuratively, thinking that she's against him instead of for him. This is the cycle that we're in.

It's become so bad that today, it's hard for a man like me to even get through to a lot of women. There are so many "grown boys" in our fatherless society that most women see me as a decoy or set-up. They see a genuine man like me trying to help, and they run from it. They can't fathom a male being caring enough to help them out. They call me a scam artist, a money hungry liar, and every name you can imagine. A lot of those women have cut off all their hair and stopped using products to enhance their beauty. Some women call themselves feminists and some call it going natural. I have met very few natural women that are positive and nice to men. For the most part, the ones that I have come into contact with are bitter and rude towards men like me. It baffles me. I assume that they have been hurt so many times by so many men that they've vowed to never trust a man again. The reason why some of them have cut off their hair in this movement, I don't know. Then I got a client that is all natural and she is happily married. She told me that she seen a study online that asked natural women why they went natural. In that study she said that over 90% of the women said because of a bad break-up. That was shocking to me but it confirmed a lot of things for me. I'm sure it is upsetting for the women who just wanted to go natural to explore natural beauty or to start fresh to be classed with the many that hate men. I honestly don't blame them, and I hurt for them. I wish there was a way that I could reach them and really show them my genuine desire to help and not hurt, but sadly, even in my profession, there are a lot of men who take advantage of these women. So I understand their pain and can only continue to do what I have been doing, and hopefully one day will be the day that they decide to heal, learn and grow.

Our women are hurting because of our neglect. Our women are hurting because of our choices. Our women are losing themselves and denying their natural essence because of our actions. Our women are degrading themselves and ruining their image and their lives because of our actions. We need our women to heal. We need our women back. We need our women to be safe in our world and in their own homes.

We need to make the decision to protect and provide for our women and stop taking advantage and hurting our women.

VIII
The Blame Game

Today we have entered into a space of irresponsibility. Men and women alike have begun to blame the opposite sex. If you ask the men, there are no good women out here. If you ask the women, there are no good men out here. I can't count how many "grown boys" I've engaged in conversations who blame all of their problems on a woman. Men claim that women are just as big of cheaters as men. Men claim that women lie just as much as men do. Men claim that women are no good and can't be trusted. Granted—for some women that is true—but for most, it's not. I know it's not true because there have been many women I've met in my lifetime who wouldn't sleep with me or even talk with me because they were in relationships. The only women who would were women that were dating "grown boys" that were cheating on them or abusing them. I have never met a woman who has a man that does everything for her and loves her with all his heart and yet, she still cheats on him. I know there may be a couple that you can think of, but that is not the majority. There are even some beautiful women who are faithful to not-so attractive men just because they have grown to love them. Then on the flip-side of that, the unattractive man may be cheating on her. It's like, man, how can you be blessed with this beautiful woman that you know you aren't accustomed to and still have the nerve to cheat? It's confusing to see the make-up of some of our relationships and how they play out.

One thing is for sure though, and that is that men need to step up and take responsibility. It is time that we accept the blame for the issues plaguing our society and do something about it. This is a high call for any man and a very long stretch for a "grown boy," but I'd like to believe that if you are reading this book, then there is a real man inside of you. I'd like to believe that you could carry the load and shoulder the responsibility of doing your part to help change society. I stopped making excuses about four years ago, and it has been amazing what I've been able to accomplish since then. I decided that I would love my wife in a way that her fa-ther didn't, and that I would help her heal her insecuri-ties and the pain of the past. I decided to wash her with love and shower her with affection and see if it would change her and make her new. She grew up without a real man in her home and the only true example she had was her mother. Although her mother was an amazing example of a human being, there were still many affir-mations that she was lacking from a male. Every woman needs that. I decided to be that person, to affirm her and let her know that she was beautiful and worthy. I stopped blaming her, judging her, critiquing her and trying to change her. I began to love her for all that she is and all that she isn't. I let her be who she is and I fostered her growth. I helped her grow. I spoke into her life in a way that would challenge her and build her up instead of tear her down. I encouraged her in a way that would motivate her and make her want more out of life and for herself. Anything she wanted to do, I supported her instead of shutting her down and making her do what I wanted or needed her to do. I made her feel like a woman and like she was loved. I saw her change before my very eyes. She stopped telling white lies out of fear that I would reprimand her or stop loving her. She stopped crying out of insecurities or inadequacies. She started to glow and to grow. Even her physical appearance changed with this newfound peace, happiness and joy. Her attitude changed and she wasn't defensive or a victim anymore. She became happy all the time and very vibrant and even more outgoing. She was already that way most of the time, but she had insecurities that would leave her crying at times. I washed those away and began to make her feel beautiful no matter what. This changed me as a man as well. It softened me up enough to open my eyes to real love. It brought me more peace and happiness because I didn't always have to question her or feel like she was out to get me. Instead, I began to feel that she was for me and I treated her as such. I gave her a place in my heart and she gladly accepted. This bond and this pure union changed my life for the better. My peace rose to a new level. My income rose to a new level. My health rose to a new level. My mind rose to a new level. I became a new man; a man that was unrecognizable to my old self and it was all because I decided to stop pointing the blame and to accept responsibility for change.

It is very important that we get to this point where we understand that we have all the power and can change the outcome. As long as we render the power to the past, we lose. However, when we accept the power in the present and realize that we can help heal a woman's heart, then our world changes. Nearly every woman you meet will have baggage; but you will have to help unpack that baggage, and please believe that she will help you unpack yours. She will mostly have a heart that's still in rehab, and you will have to be patient and nurturing to that heart to help it fully heal. There is power in these actions though. This will not only change your life but it will also change her life. You will allow this woman time to fully heal, and you can't help her without helping yourself. This will heal you as well. Then when you are pure-hearted and you both are able to start over brand new and build on a firm foundation, anything becomes possible. This is how true power couples are created. This is how real love is created and how it will last. This is at the core of those marriages that last until deaths do us part. This is real love. This needs to be the new love and the only love. There is no more time for hate and bitterness towards the opposite sex. Please forgive your mother for all the hurt she caused you. Please forgive your father for all the hurt and pain he inflicted on you. Stop allowing yourself to continue hurting and start the healing process.

Our women are not against us. Our women are not here to trick us, lie to us, and deceive us. A woman was made for love and her sole purpose for being on this Earth is to be loved, whether she's willing to admit it or not.

IX
Sex, Lies and Betrayal

As men today, we are playing a video game with the hearts of our women. Because we have been broken down and beaten by society, we are out to make others feel the pain we feel. We aren't able to trust ourselves, so we don't trust others. We don't understand what a real man is, so we live as a "grown boy." The benefits of marriage have not been shown to us, so we live our lives running from real commitment. This leads us to sex, lies and betrayal.

I remember being an early adult and not knowing who I was yet as a man. I didn't understand manhood, so I lied to myself on a daily basis. With every woman I met, my ultimate goal was to sleep with her as fast as I could. I wanted to sleep with her as fast as I could because I wanted to see how fast I could take her mind and then take her body. It was a competition. It was survival of the fittest. What has her life taught her that will keep her from falling for my games? I can count on one hand how many I was unable to con into having sex with me.

Three of those women, I met back to back. I guess it was a time in my life when God was telling me to settle down and get married. They say the 3rd is a charm. I'm not sure I'm a believer in that, but it was the 3rd one who did not fall for my con that I decided to marry. Before that, all I'd do is tell lies, have sex and betray the woman.

I can admit I was hurting. I was lost. I was confused. I wasn't a man. I thought that the more women I slept with, the more of a man I would become. It made me look like more of a man to my peers, and it made me feel like I was "the man." I remember I used to keep count of the amount of women I had sleep with. I stopped counting at 79. By that time, it all had become the same. Every woman felt just like the one before. There were no emotions, no feelings, no love, no chemistry, just sex. The sex was always the same. There wasn't much exciting about it other than the fact that I was able to outwit someone else and that my charm and deceptiveness had lured another innocent woman into bed with me. When you really think about it, it's disgusting. Be honest with yourself and ask yourself, are you that same man? Have you ever been that man? Why are you that way? I wondered the same thing.

The lies are what allow us to have sex with this unassuming woman. The sex has no meaning because we lie to get it. Then the only other option is to betray her. We came in with one real goal in mind, and that was to use her at our disposal for a little bit of pleasure and a moment to feel like more of a man; debase her in an attempt to build us up. Oftentimes while trying to play her, we end up playing ourselves. Many men lie and then sleep with a woman whom they would not marry. The next thing you know, there is a child involved. Because the relationship doesn't have a real foundation, the man walks out, and this is the betrayal. Now there's another broken woman, a man that's still empty, and a child that will be raised without a father in the home. Sex, lies and betrayal. It's a vicious cycle that we must stop. We as men have to realize what we are doing to ourselves and to our society and must become responsible enough to make the necessary changes.

What happens when we lead with lies? We play ourselves! Karma will come to us in one form or another. Either we have to pay the price, or someone we love very dearly pays the price. There comes a time when you have to decide that you are tired of the usual games and begin to change your mindset and outlook on life so that you can attract a different type of woman. Understand that sleeping with numerous women does not make you more of a man; it just confirms the fact that you are hurting and running from pain while actually creating more. This is the beginning of the cycle that affects society so negatively. Maybe this cycle has affected you in the father you didn't have or the music that shaped your culture and mindset. It all started with a lie. Our men are being lied to and then lie to our women. Then both man and woman lie to the children and the cycle continues. This is why we have found our society full of sex, lies and betrayal. Women are raising kids alone because of sex, lies and betrayal. Men are putting women in these tough positions because of the sex, lies and betrayal. It's a never-ending cycle unless you decide to stop perpetuating it. The choice is yours. It lies solely in your responsibility. If you are man enough to change the dynamic of just your family, then that could positively affect the entire world. I challenge you to take the challenge of operating in truth and maturity. Lead by example instead of by coercion and manipulation. Be the man that you were called to be and let the world begin to change because of you.

X

The Fatherless Child

As a result of the sex, lies and betrayal, many kids find themselves without fathers. Their fathers were men who didn't know what it meant to be a man. This kind of man was seeking pleasure and fulfillment without realizing that such a search would bring pain. He was trying to heal, but instead of healing, he only opened up more wounds. The consequences hit, and he dodged them by leaving this woman that he probably shouldn't have laid down with in the first place. He wasn't man enough to have a child yet, and she wasn't woman enough to help him become a man yet. They were going with the flow and fulfilling lust and now an innocent child has to pay the price. Is that child you? If so, then ask yourself, how will you be different than your father? How will you be *better* than your father? Even if your father was in the home or you saw him regularly, did he teach you everything you feel you need to know to be successful in life? If he didn't, then how will you change that? What will you do to be better than that?

There have been many studies done on the effects of not having a father in the home. Google them for yourself and do your own research. I'm not writing a research paper, but I can tell you that what you'll find is that children without fathers in the home are considered "at risk." They are considered at risk for not graduating high school, at risk of being violent, at risk of going to jail, at risk of not graduating college and so on. It's all due to the breakdown of the family structure. It takes two humans of the opposite sex to make a baby for a reason. God didn't make a mistake when he designed us that way. The male and female are almost opposites in several ways, and both sexes have a skill set that they are to pass down to their child. If a child doesn't receive the lessons from both parents, then that puts this child at a disadvantage. A woman may teach a child how to feel in the world and a man teaches a child how to be in the world. A woman teaches a child how to think in the world and a man teaches the child how to live in the world. A woman softens a child and a man toughens a child. A woman gives a child her sense of security and a man gives a child his sense of security. A child feels emotionally protected by their mother and physically protected by his father. Both parents add something to the child's life that cannot be replaced by anyone else.

A child without a father has many questions in life that lead him down a path that many dare not travel. I have spoken with many young men and women who didn't have fathers in their childhood homes, and the problems seemed to be universal. I have always been able to pinpoint two dynamics. One is the child who didn't have a father or a focused, attentive mother. The other is a child without a father but with a strong, present mother attempting to play both roles. The child without a father, who has an emotionally absent mother, struggles the most, as you may assume. My studies have shown that this child seeks for love in other places and from people who do not love him. He finds himself searching for something that should have been given to him since birth. That thing is love. He finds it in gangs, drugs, sex, music, material things and so on. He falls in love with one or more of these things, but these loves never really fulfill him all the way. He navigates through life being hurt by those he loves and by those who don't love him. As an adult, all he knows how to do is bring pain to others, but he does this without even realizing it. He is simply behaving how life has taught him to behave.

On the other hand, there is the exception to the rule. This is the child who grows up without a father but was blessed with an awesome mother. This child is taught how to survive and thrive in the world. He goes on and earns a college degree, gets a job, starts a family and leaves a legacy. How did he do it? His mother or figures in his life played a collective role, and together, they helped fill the void that his father left. Even with that being the case, I have spoken with several young men in those shoes who said they wondered all their lives why their fathers never loved them. They wondered why their fathers left them. They wondered all their lives if they would ever be good enough to receive their fathers' love. It put a sense of urgency in them that made them never want to do that to their own children. Some of those young men become excellent fathers because of what happened to them. It would be our hope that this is how every man would be affected by not having a father, but unfortunately, it's not the case.

My point in this section is to reach you if you are a father who is not present in your child's life. First ask yourself why. Whatever the reason, begin to identify steps to eliminate that reason and find a way to change it. I want you to understand that your child is at risk for the wrong paths in life, and you can do something about it. You can stop your child from being abused by the world. You can stop your child from hurting and causing pain to others. You can save your child from the penitentiary and teach your child how to thrive in this world. Please realize that no matter what you accomplish in your own life, none of it will matter if your child grows up and says that you weren't a good father. If your child can grow up and say that you weren't a good father then you have failed as a man. It is never too late to right your wrongs. If you are reading this, then you have time. You have time to make it right. Undo the wrong you've done. Swallow your pride and become a man for your child's sake.

Did you hurt your child's mother? Remember the quote: "The best thing a man can do for his kids is to love their mother!" I can't remember who said it, but it holds a lot of weight. You teach your child how to love and how to treat others by how you treat your child's mother. If your child hears you talking nasty about his mother or cursing her out, then how do you think that will affect your child? Do you think he will grow up loving and kind if all he has seen or heard is you cursing and belittling the person that loves him the most? This isn't about you. This is about your child. This is bigger than you and your child's mother. This is about your child's life. Get over whatever it is between you and the mother of your child so that you can be a positive influence in your child's life. If you need to make up with your child's mother but you don't know how, then just write up this letter below and put it in the mail to her. If she doesn't hear you the first time, then send it to her every week until she gives in! I want you to know that a woman is made for love and if you are genuine and sincere, you can wash her with love, and for the child's sake she will let you be a father to your child. How long it takes depends on how much wrong you have done to her and how much wrong she has suffered in her life. Be patient, but be persistent.

Here's the letter:

Hey _____,

I wanted to write you to get some things off of my chest. I know right now your face is twisted in a way indescribable. You're probably wondering what on Earth made me sit down and handwrite a letter to you. Well, to be honest, I've finally had an epiphany. I realize that all the hate and pain in our world comes from men doing just what I've been doing. I've been hurt and I spread that hurt. I've been carrying a grudge against others and against you. I've made mistakes and ran from the consequences many times and then got mad at the people who tried to hold me accountable for my actions. I know that there may have been some things that you've done to me that really hurt me or confused me, but I realize that you've been through some pain in your life too. We hurt others only because we are hurting ourselves. I want to make it right with you. I want to accept responsibility for my actions so that I can play a real role in my child's life. I don't want my child to grow up and one day and say that I wasn't there for him. I want my child to know that even though you and I couldn't work it out, I still was man enough to take care of him because he's my responsibility. I'm sorry for all the hurt and pain I've caused. It's my fault. I accept full responsibility, and I apologize for that from the bottom of my heart. Tell me what you need and what I can do to really have a bigger role in my child's life. I'm ready to take that step, and I won't let you down this time. I hope to hear from you very soon!

Sincerely,

―――――――――――

Write up that letter and word it to fit your situation. Make sure that you point no blame on the woman no matter what she did to you. If she cheated on you, if she lied to you, if she stole from you, if she lied on you, if she left you, no matter what she did, please know that there is a reason behind it that is much bigger than you. Forgive her for any pain that she's caused and accept responsibility for everything! I promise you that this will break her down and open her up. She's made for love. Just make sure that when she opens up and lets you in, that you won't take advantage of her kindness. Her kindness isn't her weakness; it's her strength. I need you to be as strong as her and be kind too. This is bigger than you, and your child needs you. Your child's mother needs you. If she was good enough to sleep with, then she is good enough for you to help take care of. Pay your child support! Give more than you're supposed to give. Give more than you can. Accept full responsibility for your actions and I promise you that good will come back to you. It will pay off. That very child, who you man up to take care of, could be the one that retires you one day. I've seen it happen many times. That child growing up and being successful will mean more to you than anything in the world. Do what you have to do and be there for your child. No more excuses. I don't want to hear them. The world doesn't want to hear them. Stop making excuses and start making changes. The world needs you! Your child needs you!

Even if your child is grown and there is no child support to be paid, take the time to reach out to your child. I can't count how many adults have testified that their life became whole when their long lost fathers took the time to reach out to them before he left this world. One conversation could heal the pain they've felt all their lives. If one conversation doesn't heal their pain, then keep going. One conversation should not be your goal. Seek to build and sustain a relationship with your child. Understand that there may be a lot of hate, resentment and pain built up inside of your child, and it's your responsibility to work through it. You have to keep finding a way to reach your child. If they are hurting because of you, then it's your job to make it right. Do it for your child. Do it for yourself.

NO CHILD LEFT BEHIND!!

XI
When a Man Finds a Woman

Very few men understand the importance of a woman in our lives. A man is taught to believe that if he has countless women, he is more of a man. I have come to realize that that's one of the biggest lies we've been told about manhood. I was 21 years old when I found my wife. In so many ways, she changed my life. Until that point, I was lost and confused about life. I didn't know who I was or who I wanted to become. I was sleeping with a different girl every week and sometimes 3-5 women a week. I was lost and hurting. Then finally, I found a woman that loves and respects herself, and I began to see women completely differently. I realized that one woman is enough. I realized that she was created to be loved and cherished, not used and abused. This revelation was life changing in itself.

When I met her, I was selling drugs, skipping classes and wandering aimlessly. I was a mess. While getting to know her, I expressed my deepest thoughts and desires, and my revelations clicked in her spirit some-where. She held onto the dreams that I had expressed and she held me to them. We grew serious in our rela-tionship, and she loved me with her everything. She knew I wanted to write a book, so after I began to write that book, she invested in me and gave me $1,600 to publish my first book at the age of 22. She knew that I was smarter than a drug dealer and that I had too much to offer the world to squander it in the streets. She de-manded that I choose between her and the street life. I tried to force her hand and choose the street life, and she kept her word and left me. I realized that she was only doing that for my own good and for our family. I begged her back and I left the streets alone. She stood her ground in such a way that I couldn't get away with lies and living a life with low moral value. She made me elevate my lifestyle and my mindset in order to be with her. Her strength would change me forever.

With this woman in my life, I became more of a man. She supported my endeavors that were in line with my purpose, and if they weren't, she would let me know how she felt. Her standing her ground and forcing me to step up or step out changed my life. It was she who launched my career as an author, speaker and life coach. She would not accept less. She refused to be with a deadbeat man who didn't want more out of life than fast money, fast cars and fast women. She wanted a man who knew his purpose and was not afraid to fulfill it. Today, I'm writing this book as a 29-year-old man who is one of the top life coaches in the world. I am highly connected and widely known. I'm getting bookings from around the globe and making more money than I could have ever imagined or dreamed. A large part of my success is because I found a good woman, and I allowed her to be that woman. I did not fight to change her into less of a woman. I did not try to strip her of her self-worth and self-respect. I let her be who God intended for her to be.

So often, we as men find good women and ruin them because we aren't ready or willing to change. We ruin their lives because we want to do what feels comfortable instead of what is right. We fight to change these women and to weaken them. We try everything to break women down so that they will allow us to be sorry excuses for men. That's not what a woman is meant to be. That's not why God made her. God made her to hold a man up. God made her to make a man better. God made her to be a man's backbone, his rib cage, his support system, not his footstool. We have to allow her to be what God intended for her to be. A good woman can change your life if you let her. Let her be an asset to your life instead of turning her into a liability. She wants more out of you and more for you, so allow it to be. She wants you to be faithful, so be a man and be faithful. She wants you to be ambitious, so be a man and be ambitious. She wants you to be responsible, so be a man and be responsible. She wants you to succeed, because if you succeed, then she succeeds as well. But if you break her, she may lose her essence. If you break her, then she will fail at her job and allow you to fail at yours. If you break her, then she will become an enabler. If you fight her until she gives in, then you have lost a good woman. When you do this, she's no longer a real woman; now she's a puppet. Is that what you really want? A puppet? Do you really want a doormat for a wife? Do you really want a doorknob for a wife? Is that what you are really looking for? Or do you want a woman who can be your backbone when you're weak? Do you want a woman who can be your eyes when you're blind? Do you want a woman who can hold your house together when you're falling apart?

When you find a good woman, please understand that she can take your life to the next level and allow her to do so. She's created to love you. She's created to enhance your life. She's created to be the best thing that will happen to you. Allow this woman to be a woman. Be man enough to grow and go to the next level of life. Do not break her just because growth and maturity are uncomfortable for you. Do not break her just because you don't want to be faithful, loving, responsible, compassionate and understanding. My wife changed my life, and I know there's a woman who can do the same thing for you. Allow her to be what God intended for her to be.

XII
The Benefits of Marriage

I can't express enough how important marriage is for us as men. Marriage is everything. You may not agree, but I want you to really ask yourself why. Why don't you want to be married? Let me guess. You don't feel it changes anything. You don't feel you should get married just to have sex with a woman. You aren't ready to get married because you still have living to do. You don't think you can be faithful to one woman. You aren't ready to be locked down. Commitment scares you. " 'Til death do us part" are words that frighten you to your core. You don't know if she's the one. You don't believe in marriage. You've never seen a successful example of marriage. No one you know is married and happy. The married people you know hate it and wish they were in your shoes.

I hear you! But I don't feel you. I once thought the same way. Well, I'll take that back. I'm not sure if I ever thought that deeply about marriage. I wanted marriage. I didn't know if I could be faithful. I didn't know if I was ready. I didn't know if I really loved her with all my heart. Deep down, I just wanted to be in right standing with God. I wanted God's grace, favor and mercy on my life. I wanted to get out of sin. That was my heart's desire. No, I wasn't a holy roller. No, I didn't go to church every Sunday. No I didn't quote scriptures all day or speak in tongues. I just knew that God was the creator of love and the institution of marriage and that it was a holy union and seen as right in His eyes. I wanted to be seen as right in God's eyes. If you don't believe in God, then you have a totally different case. If you don't fear God, then I fear for you. If you don't honor God, then I'm praying for you.

There are so many benefits to marriage; almost too many to list. First and foremost, marriage brings favor over your life because you are in alignment to receive your blessings. You have eliminated one of the most commons sins and that's fornication. Next, marriage can bring clarity if you are willing to be faithful. Marriage can bring focus that is beyond your understanding. If you become a man and you commit your life to your wife and your family, then marriage is the absolute greatest creation ever known to mankind.

Before I got married, I was a drug dealer, a womanizer, a liar, a cheater, a thief, a manipulator, a punk, a phony, a wannabe, a loser, and a lost and wandering boy. I had no real strength. I had swag. I had women. I had nice clothes and a nice car. I had good looks and a great body. I had everything on the outside, but I had nothing on the inside. I had no real character and integrity. I had no real money or success. I had no real peace or happiness.

Then when I got married and decided to be faithful, all of my extra energy that once would go into juggling several other women transferred to renewing myself. When I wasn't focused on my wife and my son, I was focused on my business and my purpose. This type of direct focus would change my life. It's hard to put into words how divine it is to be married and faithful.

Please understand that this message is from a man who had slept with over 100 beautiful women by the age of 22. This message is from a man who would regularly sleep with 3 women in one day. This message is from a man who never heard the word 'no' from a woman I liked until I met my wife. So please don't think this message is from a guy who never got a woman and couldn't get women and just desired marriage so that I could finally have one woman all to myself. That's not the case. I had all the women, and I had so many women that I supplied all my friends and even some enemies with women. What most men fantasized about, I actually lived. I'm here to tell you that it's not all that you think it will be. It's an empty lifestyle. I did not feel complete until I got married and was faithful.

In my marriage, I slipped up a couple times and got caught up into other women, but they weren't comfortable places or anywhere I wanted to remain. After those two times that my eyes really wandered farther than I wanted them to, I snapped out of it and never went down that road again. Today, I'm 100% faithful and I do not entertain other women. There are some that still come at me daily. There have been women who have tried to pen me in corners. There have been women who would hit on me during a life-coaching session or text me pictures and explicit text messages. They come and they come hard, but marriage is so fulfilling because I'm upholding my end of the bargain, so I don't want to give that up.

There's no greater feeling than to know that you are man enough to be with one woman. There's no greater feeling than to know that you have enough discipline and have mastered your will enough to control yourself in any situation. That's real manhood. That takes real discipline, integrity and character. To be honest, it feels good to have a wife who is coveted by thousands of women but not one of them can be her. You have leverage in any situation when you have real discipline and self-control. This type of discipline and self-control takes your life and your business to another level.

I'm a 29-year-old black man from a low-income family. Only a couple guys I knew growing up went on to be successful, and those who did, it was because of their athletic abilities. I'm not sure what will become of them after they pass their prime in sports. Only time will tell. Outside of athletes, I don't know anyone with massive success that I can look up to and emulate. I look around and I don't see or meet black men under the age of 30 years old who make six figures by fulfilling their purpose. I have 17 avenues of income. I have two for-profit companies and two non-profit companies. I have content in almost every form of media. I just turned 29 a few days ago. I have a peace, happiness, and family life, focus and grind that I haven't seen in anyone to my age. I meet guys who have money, but they have no real peace and happiness. I meet guys who have peace and happiness, but they don't have time for a family. I meet guys who have families, but they don't have grind.

I'M NO BETTER THAN ANY OTHER MAN!!!

I have simply made different choices than most men. When I look at the men I meet and I compare their lives to mine, if I have more money, peace and happiness than them, it's usually because of one thing. They don't have a real relationship with God. What I mean is that they don't live by God's principles. They don't fear, respect or wholeheartedly honor God. Therefore, they are not dedicated to the women in their lives. They are cheating on their girlfriends or cheating on their wives. They have no real moral code or they think they know it all and are too smart to believe in God wholeheartedly. They are lost.

That is the main difference that I always notice. Guys ask me, How did you become so successful so young? How did you do all of this without a college degree? How did you get the gigs you got and the brand that you have? My answer is that I found balance. I dedicated my life to Christ and to the purpose that he has for me. I'm 100% faithful to my wife. I don't drink. I don't smoke. I don't curse. I don't club. I don't watch pornography. I don't masturbate. I don't envy my neighbor. I don't hate. I'm not trivial, backstabbing or phony. I'm not conniving, greedy and deceptive. I don't have an agenda or ulterior motives. I live 100% transparent and as pure as I can possibly live.

DO I MAKE MISTAKES??? YES!!!! I occasionally lust after a big butt that passes me. A big butt or a nice set of thighs is my weaknesses. Do I approach her? Absolutely not! Do I send someone else to get her number? Absolutely not! If I meet her at a seminar or through work, do I make a pass at her? Absolutely not! Because I don't act on what I may sometimes feel, I believe it keeps my life in balance and God continues to bless my efforts.

IT IS NOT MY WORKS THAT HAS SAVED ME! It's God's grace and my willingness and commitment to fulfill my purpose on this Earth. So if you want more money, peace, happiness, love, respect and honor, then I suggest that you evaluate your life and eliminate everything that is working against you. Remove all crutches, hindrances, vices and weaknesses. Fight daily to become a better man. Don't get stuck in a life of mediocrity. Don't do what every other man is doing. Even me; writing this is strengthening me, and I know the attack and the traps set around my life after writing this will be greater. I know women from my past will try to make something out of nothing or try to come back into my life to test my commitment. I know women will try to get close to me and catch me with my guards down to try and take my strength like Delilah did Sampson in the Bible. I know she is coming. I know the tests are coming. I am preparing as we speak. I'm thinking and planning as we speak.

I urge you to settle down so that your life can rise up. I urge you to find true happiness, peace and love. Love the woman in your life. Get married if you aren't, and be 100% faithful to one woman. I guarantee you that if you love one woman with your all, remain faithful to her and then give all other energy to fulfilling your purpose; it will change your life drastically. You won't recognize the person you have become. I scratch my head daily at the success I have been able to experience. But then I realize that I could not have seen an increase in my life if I never found order in my life. Get order in your life so that God can send an increase. Get aligned so that you can receive the blessings that are intended for you. Man up and settle down! Your future, and ultimately your life, is depending on it. Make better choices and you will see better results. Stop looking at the success of others and basing your life on how you think they may be living. Yes, they may have money and fame, but that doesn't mean that they have peace and happiness. Now you've just received a message from someone who has peace, happiness and success, and I've told you how I got it. I dare you to try it with commitment, and I guarantee that if you stick to it, you will see results. It didn't happen overnight for me. It has been six years that I've been on this journey as a married man. It didn't happen overnight, but it did happen. I guarantee you that if you love yourself enough to commit and that if you love your wife enough to be faithful and God enough to surrender to His will, then your life will be changed.

XIII
The Next Generation

What will we pass on? If we can embrace marriage, and embrace real love, then we change the culture in our world. We have to ask ourselves what the next generation will be like for our kids. Ask yourself if you want your son to be drug dealer. Ask yourself if you want your daughter to be a prostitute in any form. If the answer is no, then you have to commit to doing something about it. You maybe can't change the whole world, but you can change the lineage in your family. You can shift the atmosphere for those who will come after you, and as your beliefs are passed down, each person that embraces them will spread them even further. We have to think about the next generation. We have to prepare the world for them to live in it. Don't get so caught up in your life and your happiness that you forget that your kids must live on well after you're gone. Right now, our generation and the immediate generation after us seems very lost. There are elementary kids having sex already. There are 5th graders who are pregnant and cursing. Kids are doing drugs and smoking weed in middle school. Kids are carrying guns to school when they are too weak to even brace the backfire of the gun. We see little girls barely strong enough in the legs to walk but already booty dancing. Little boys are grabbing their crotches and sagging their pants. You maybe can't change the world, but you can touch some lives. You can open your mouth and say something. You can impact your own children and they will impact their friends, and all of them will impact their own children. That is how we begin to prepare the next generation. That is how we begin to repair our world.

If we are content with the way things are right now, then our children might not live to see 50 years old. We may have to bury our kids before we are buried. Our youth are out of control, and it's claiming lives. We need men who will stand up and say something. The world needs real men. It's timeout for grown men sitting on the sidelines doing nothing. I'm tired of seeing men in their mid-30's still thinking like teenage boys. There is more to life than spending money and getting girls. We must accept that and pass that knowledge on to positively affect the next generation.

If we cultivate a society full of love, then we change our future. When we as men step up to the plate and commit faithfully to our women, get married, start families, and raise our kids in two-parent households, then our world begins to change. If you came up in a single-parent home, imagine how much stress you would have saved there had been two whole and healthy parents in the home. Don't you want that for your kids? There is strength in numbers and we need our other half. We need strong women by our sides and to instill real values into our kids. The next generation will benefit greatly from our stability. I asked myself, what is the root of all evil? The answer was a lack of love. Love conquers all. If a person has true love, there is no need to steal, kill or destroy. If a person has real love, there is no reason to hate others. Love will cut down on crime, on teen pregnancies, on abortion, on hate, on discrimination and all of the things that plague our society. We need real love, and when we get it, we must pass it down.

XIV
Building Business

This is so important for a man. As I say all the time, if you won't build your dream, then someone else will hire you to help build theirs. It is very important that we understand that we were born millionaires and we just need to cash out on our dreams. As men, we equate our net-worth to our self-worth. The less money we make, the less we feel about ourselves. Although money is important to have, that is a huge mistake. We have to learn that business building is important, but it's not everything. So many of us get stuck on someone else's job, and we build and sustain their dreams and then neglect our own. Each one of us was born with a unique set of gifts that can set us apart from every other man. Not everyone who reads this book can write a book, so that separates me. I can't do half the things other men can do, so that separates them. There is a gift inside of you and it needs to be brought out. If you have tried it and you've had any type of success at it and you actually love it, then it's worth trying hard at it. No matter how good you are, if you aren't diligently trying to get better, then you won't get very far.

Identify your natural gifts:

There are gifts that you possess already that can change your life. There are things you can do that not everyone around you can do. You have to identify those gifts and/or passions and turn them into business. I'll paint a picture for you so you know what I mean. In the fourth grade we had to write an essay, and my teacher chose only my essay to read to the entire class. That was a sign about my mind. She then told my parents that I was gifted and needed to be challenged more. As a result, I was placed in the gifted class. As I grew older, I began to write poetry. It just flowed. I could write about anything and make it rhyme and make perfect sense. I didn't know any other student in my class or grade who could do it as well as I could. The gift of words was following me around. I ignored it, but it was always there. It was something that I could do that not everyone else could. I wasn't the best writer in the world, but I had a leg up on the competition around me. Look at me today. You are reading my written words, so I guess the gift paid off.

Give your gifts a purpose:

It's one thing to identify your gifts, but it's something totally different to be able to give them a purpose. How can you use the gift to make the lives of others better?

Can you bring knowledge to them? Can you bring peace to them? Can you bring convenience to them? Can you bring laughter to them? Can you bring entertainment to them? What can your gift do for others to make their lives just a little bit easier? I decided at the age of 22 to use my gift of writing to put some of my wisdom down on paper. I haven't stopped. After I wrote the book, I started putting my wisdom into quotes and posting them online. Then I started putting them into videos. One thing led to the next, and today, I've reached millions and millions of people with my words of wisdom. My products sell in over 70 countries and 6 different continents. Lord willing, I have another 50 years of work to do. I decided to use my gift, not to edify myself, but to lift up others. I want to make your life easier by sharing my knowledge and wisdom about life. I know that God was gracious enough to let me live through the things I have and grant me the wisdom He has, so it's my duty to share it. I want you to do the same with your gift. No matter the gift, you can give it a purpose and make the lives of those around you better in some way.

Build A Brand:

Don't just use your gifts; brand your gifts. Find a lane and claim that lane. Give yourself a title or a slogan for your business and stick with it. Let people get to know you for your gifts. The Bible says that your gifts will make room for you. Be ready for the room you will receive. Get online in every area that you can and lock down your lane. Use all of the free social media tools; stay consistent with your material, and your brand will begin to build itself like that. Today, people know me as a motivator and life coach because I stick to what I know. I want to comment on sports sometimes, but I'm not a sports commentator, so I stay away from it. I want to crack jokes sometimes, but I'm not a comedian, so I stay away from it. I coach life and I do it well, so I stick to it. Many people never get known for doing one thing well because they attempt to do too many things too soon. You can dabble in many things, but do one thing well first, and then you can expand the brand. A brand is essential to being remembered for what you did in the world. It will form itself if you stick to what you do really well for long enough. Whatever the people reinforce, that is a sign to which you should take heed. I'm known mostly for relationship advice because when I tweet relationship quotes, they get the most retweets. Being that the people loved those tweets more than anything else I shared, I kept doing that and it grew my following exponentially. Today when I'm called in to speak by colleges or organizations, it's mostly for relationship seminars. I'm okay with that because that is my strongest area, and that is how I have branded myself.

Expand the brand:

You don't have to just do one thing. From your main gift, there will be other ways that you can use that gift and fulfill purpose while simultaneously making a profit. It is important that you tap out all of your gifts so that you leave nothing undiscovered inside of you when it's time to check out of this world. For example, I started as an author but then from there, I became a speaker, relationship coach, screenwriter, ghostwriter, author consultant, film/TV producer, life coach and teacher. Today, I have 17 streams of income, and they are all purposed-based. One thing led to the next. When I was working for someone else, I made approximately $1,200-$1,800 a month. Now I make that or more in a day because I've tapped into my natural gifts and expanded my brand. Today as I'm writing this, I have received a $1,000 check from a reality TV show, $500 from a student taking my life coach training course, $99 from a student taking my Birth Your Book training class, a royalty check from my last book that is available as an eBook, and a few other checks from sources that I can't quite remember. I sit back, scratch my head sometimes and wonder how I got here, but I know it is because I decided to live 100% for Christ and to use my natural gifts with which He blessed me.

I don't have a college degree. I don't have any formal training. I don't have any formal certificates. But, I make well into the six-figure range and I work 100% for myself. This has made me so much happier and brought so much peace and joy to my life. I wake up knowing that I don't have to punch anyone's clock, that the work I've put in will pay off and the more work I put in, the more it will pay off. I can smile when I look to the future, knowing that it can only get better from here. All I can do is grow if I'm willing to keep going. I don't write any of this to impress you. I write all of this to impress upon you that if a young country boy who loves Jesus can do this then so can you!

If we have more men willing to sacrifice, grind and take chances on themselves, then we would have more men being fulfilled in their lives and happier on this Earth. We need motivated men because motivated men will make good husbands and good fathers. And if we have good husbands and good fathers, then our world will change for the better.

Your first business is to fall in love with your creator and to align yourself with his Holy Bible. If you do that with a pure and genuine heart, then you will not know failure from that point on. Even in the struggles, you will find peace. Even in the famines, you will find food. Even in the droughts, you will find water. There are no recessions for those who wholeheartedly serve God. I wouldn't write it if it weren't so. That has been my saving grace. I was trying to live life and build business without the owner's manual, but when I tapped into it, my life changed drastically.

XV
Leaving a Legacy

What will you do that will outlive you? Live your life in such a way that people will carry your name on after you are gone. The only people we care to remember are those who served the world to make it a better place. Legacy must become everything to a man. If only your children carry your legacy, that is enough for the world. If your children carry your legacy, then their children will carry it as well and it will forever be alive and impacting our world.

Many men have been tricked to believe that life is about working our fingers to the bone so that we can acquire a four-bedroom house on a lake, a corvette, boat, 401k and retirement plan. We can gain all of that, live a life that seems fulfilling, die and then be forgotten. Life is much more than what you can acquire while you are here. Life is about what you are able to leave on Earth that is intangible and can live on. As I was growing up, my mother would always say: *I've never seen a U-Haul hooked up to a hearse*. What she meant is that when you leave, you can't take anything with you. You came in naked and you will leave naked.

So why are we here? Are we here simply to live and die? Are we here to just pass through life just to say we did? No, we are all born into this world to leave it better than it was when we came. We all acquire knowledge and wisdom along our journey and it's just as unique as our fingerprints. No matter who came before you or who will come after you, no one will think exactly like you do. That means that it's your duty to leave some wisdom for the world. I urge you today to identify a non-profit organization that you can start. Identify a book that you can write. Identify some life lessons you can teach your kids that they will never forget. Identify some needs in our world that you can meet. If you have done all of that already, then you are well on your way to leaving a lasting impression on our world. I urge you to do more though. Find young men who seem like they are hungry for success, and teach them the real definition of success. Teach them that the "American Dream" could actually become their nightmare if they aren't very careful. Teach them about purpose and legacy. You see, great leaders don't just lead. Great leaders build up other leaders as well. If there is anything that I can do to help anyone who is investing in himself and trying his best to make something happen, then I do it. Don't just be a leader; build leaders.

XVI
What Can We Do

The Final Call:

I'm calling all men who read this book to take action. Become a better man. Do not settle for mediocrity, but strive to be better than any man you have ever met. Understand what a real man is and why you are here. Know that manhood is about accepting responsibility and not running from it. Being a man is about loving our women and our children and working tirelessly to make our world a better place. Become a master of yourself, and you will be able to master this life. Think outside of yourself and serve a God that is bigger than you and He will show you a purpose for your life that is bigger than you.

I have made all of the mistakes that a man can make. I have been through the lowest of lows and the worst of the worst. I didn't know how I ended up there, but I did know that I couldn't stay there! I changed my life and started being a real man. I know that no matter where you are in your journey, there is still help. If you've been a deadbeat dad, you can turn it around. If you've been an abusive partner, you can turn it around. If you've been a criminal and menace to society, you can turn it around. If you're feeling lost, you can be found. I know because I've been all of those things, but look at me now.

We can make a difference. We can change the world. We can do more than our fathers did. We can shock the world. We can come together and be a coalition instead of being in competition. Let go of the shady business practices. Let go of the "crab in the barrel" mentality. Let go of the "dog eat dog" mentality and become a real man in every sense of the word.

It is not my wish to be "the man" to all men. It is not my wish to be looked up to by other men. It is not my wish to be the ONE. It's my wish to inspire my brother to be better than he is right now. It's my wish to inspire my brother to seek greatness instead of settling for mediocrity. If we help each other, then we can't fail.

Find your woman and love her with everything in you. Grab your kids and love them with everything in you. Look to God and love Him with everything in you. Look trials and tribulations in the eye and laugh at them. Be courageous because we were meant to be courageous.

OUR WORLD NEEDS REAL MEN!!!

Note from the Author

I want to thank you for reading this book, typos and all. I really just wanted to come from my heart and not from my mind. Sometimes we try so hard to be politically correct that the truth is never told. I wanted this book to just be real so that real change can come from it. Please don't take offense to anything that I've written. It was all written from love. I tried to use myself as an example as much as possible because I want it to be clear that I've lived what I teach about.

Please take what you can get from this book and leave what's not for you. Everything isn't meant to be for everyone and truthfully this book may only be relevant to a small group of men. If it's not for you please pass it along to someone that it is for. Thank you so very much for your support! I hope that one day I can return the favor to you.

Much love,
Tony A. Gaskins Jr.
tony@tonygaskins.com
booktony@tonygaskins.com
www.TonyGaskins.com

Made in the USA
Charleston, SC
08 July 2013

20385384R00067